Your Church and the Law

David Parrott is Continuing Ministerial Education Adviser in the Diocese of Chelmsford and honorary Education Adviser to the Ecclesiastical Law Society.

Your Church and the Law

A simple explanation and guide

David Parrott

CANTERBURY
PRESS
Norwich

© David Parrott 2008
First published in 2008 by the Canterbury Press Norwich
(a publishing imprint of Hymns Ancient & Modern Limited,
a registered charity)
13–17 Long Lane, London EC1A 9PN

www.scm-canterburypress.co.uk

British Library Cataloguing in Publication data

A catalogue record for this book is available
from the British Library

ISBN 978-1-85311-927-9

Typeset by Regent Typesetting, London
Printed in the UK by CPI William Clowes
Beccles NR34 7TL

Contents

Foreword

I warmly commend this very practical guide for all those who love and serve the Church of England. But the very word 'law' will put off some. Have we not done away with the law in favour of gospel, as with Paul in Romans? Apart from this being a wrong way to read what Paul meant by 'Torah' – the identity of God's *ancient* people – an anti-nomian attitude also dangerously fails to do justice to what the New Testament says about God's *new* people – the Christian church. A 'people' have customs, laws, commitments. A 'covenant' speaks of contract. A 'body' is about the relationship of differing organs. A 'house' or 'temple' implies plans and structure. 'Branches' imply organic relationship. 'Bride' tells us of commitment, love and intimacy. 'Communion' is having something in common. All these metaphors for the church in the New Testament reflect an *ordered* church. Law reflects that order. Paul tells us that 'all things should be done decently and in order' (1 Cor. 14.40). The original word here means in sequence, according to proper procedure, in an orderly manner, according to an assigned arrangement or administration.

David Parrott's 'simple explanation and guide' to our church and the law shows us how to be such a Pauline, Anglican and 'ordered' church.

†Christopher Guildford
July 2008

Abbreviations

AMP	Annual Meeting of Parishioners
APCM	Annual Parochial Church Meeting
CDM	Clergy Discipline Measure
CME	Continuing Ministerial Education
CPAS	Church Pastoral Aid Society
CPO	Child Protection Officer
CRB	Criminal Records Bureau
CRR	Church Representation Rules
CTE	Churches Together in England
DAC	Diocesan Advisory Committee
DCPA	Diocesan Child Protection Adviser
DPC	Data Protection Commissioner
EIG	Ecclesiastical Insurance Group
ELS	Ecclesiastical Law Society
LEP	Local Ecumenical Partnership
NSM	Non-Stipendiary Minister
OLM	Ordained Local Minister
PCC	Parochial Church Council
PTO	Permission to Officiate
SSM	Self-Supporting Minister
TEN	Temporary Events Notice

I

Introduction

For some time the Ecclesiastical Law Society (ELS) has been wanting to exercise its educational purpose by publishing material that will be useful to clergy and others to help them to understand and work with church law. As their Education Adviser I have taken on the project and this book is the result. I am grateful to the Chairman of the ELS and other members of the Executive Committee for their help and encouragement while I have been working on it.

One of the leading Roman Catholic canonists, James A. Coriden, writes, 'Canon law shapes and guides the life of the church in many ways. For those who care about the church, it is important to understand its rules.'[1] It is a care for the church held by the ELS and by this author that drives this work. Mission, evangelism, vision and leadership are in many ways more important than church law, but for any minister or PCC member to be effective they must to some degree master the law that affects and bounds the ministry and mission of the church.

This book is not first and foremost a pastoral guide, although it contains much pastoral advice along the way. Its prime task is to set out the law (both the law of the church and the law of the land) which is relevant to the church's work, so that those involved in churches can act within the legal framework. It is aimed at clergy, readers, churchwardens, PCC members, bishops, archdeacons, diocesan officers, and anyone who works and ministers in the church and needs to know the law within which they function.

It is not intended to be the last word, but seeks to get you going, direct you to other resources, and help you to ask the right

---

1 Coriden, *An Introduction to Canon Law*, p. 6.

questions. I am not attempting to give all the answers, but to help you to know how to find them. That is because there are simply too many questions, and the answers always depend on the exact circumstances. When I teach law to clergy I do not try to teach people to know the answer to all the issues that can arise. It is more important to know that there is a question to be asked. Anyone dipping into this book will quickly find that there are more issues than any of us could hold in mind. But if you know enough to be alert to the issues, you can come back to the detail when a specific question arises.

Each chapter follows a pattern of headings. First there is a small scenario. This is intended to whet your appetite. It gives a simple example of a situation that could arise in which there are legal issues. The chapter does not answer the scenario specifically, but looks more broadly at the issues. There is then a brief section under the heading 'What you need to know'. This sets out the key legal issues relevant to the chapter subject. The following two sections, 'FAQs' and 'What happens when ...' pick up on practical examples and questions. I am grateful to a large number of clergy and colleagues who have suggested questions and issues to include in these sections. Next, if there are specific legal resources these are listed. Finally, under 'Links', I have tried to add some web-sites which could be useful for further information. If life gets very difficult you may need to find yourself an expert (your diocesan secretary, archdeacon or registrar) but you can go a long way towards helping yourself by doing a bit of research.

The terms 'ecclesiastical law' and 'canon law' are not easy to define. Others have tackled the problem of distinguishing the terms.[2] For the purposes of this work I shall use the term 'church law', except where another term is specifically necessary in the context.

You may notice that I frequently use the term 'minister' in the text. This is the term used in the Canons of the Church of England and it avoids some of the issues around distinctions of gender and between priest and deacon. When the canons talk about

---

2 For example, Doe, *The Legal Framework of the Church of England*, pp. 12–16.

incumbent responsibilities they often then say the 'minister with the cure of souls'. Again I shall follow that convention.

A number of people have read material for me including Rupert Bursell, Gerald Funnell, Gillian Harrison, Lindsay Yates, Will Adam, Judith Brooks, Jean Halliday, Steven Webb, and Tony Boon. My thanks to them, although any errors remain my responsibility.

Finally my thanks go to my wife Sue, whose patience and encouragement have enabled me to carry on with this project.

2

Why Does the Church Need Laws?

What you need to know

Why do we need church law?

Imagine a group of teenagers playing football on a grassy cliff-top. At the edge of the cliff is a fence. It marks a boundary beyond which it is not safe to go. Those playing football know that it is deeply unwise to go beyond the fence, or even to run towards it at high speed. So they don't. The fence does not help them in their game of football; it does not tell them the purpose of football; it does not enhance the game itself in any significant way: but it does keep them safe from harm and show them where are the limits beyond which lies danger.[1] In some ways this image applies to church law. It sets a safe boundary within which we can operate as a church. However, we need to go a little further in our initial exploration.

Norman Doe explores the complex purposes of church law and concludes: 'The purpose of ecclesiastical regulation can be identified by determining the intention of its makers. General theories of purpose are fundamentally classifications of intent.'[2] He reaches this conclusion through exploring two theories of church law: the facility theory and the order theory.[3] The facility theory relates to the intention to permit, allow or encourage some action or behaviour. The function of regulation in this theory is to serve the purposes for which the church exists. In the order theory the

---

1 My thanks to Archdeacon Peter Taylor for this image.

2 Doe, *The Legal Framework of the Church of England*, p. 52.

3 These two theories are from the study of Roman Catholic canon law.

focus is on regulation as disciplinary or coercive. He concludes that the Church of England has employed both theories in various pieces of legislation. Mark Hill states this slightly differently when he says: 'The purpose of the law ... is to regulate the functioning of the Church and the conduct of its component members by a combination of commands, prohibitions and permissions.'[4]

Both these writers are talking about the need for order in the church based on a purpose in the minds of the legislators. It is interesting to see how theory and practice come together when addressing a current issue in church law. At a recent conference of the Ecclesiastical Law Society on the subject of Law in the Anglican Communion, Gregory Cameron[5] described attitudes in the church as motivated by either ardour or order. He went on to speak of the divisions in the Anglican Communion that are rooted in an emphasis on the theme of ardour. He described the 'ardour of the left', which seeks to loosen the restrictions of church law to allow a greater 'inclusiveness', and the 'ardour of the right', which is prepared to override traditional understandings of jurisdiction in the defence of 'orthodoxy'. There are those who would say that order is vital to the church and to its common communion and others who argue that their ardour takes precedence over order. Ultimately both positions leave us in disarray unless we are able to understand the nature of law and order and keep it in balance with the primary purposes of the church. Cameron concludes: 'Ardour without order in the life of the church would result in chaos; but order without ardour would result in empty formalism.'[6]

It can be seen that clergy, readers, churchwardens and others need to have some understanding of the purpose of church law, and how to live in the balance between ardour and order.

Let me tackle this from another angle. All laws govern relationships. Family law governs the relationship between family members in good times and in bad. Civil law governs the relationships we have with our neighbours and those we interact with day by

---

4 Hill, *Ecclesiastical Law*, p. 2.
5 Deputy Secretary General of the Anglican Communion.
6 Gregory Cameron, 'Ardour and Order', *Ecclesiastical Law Journal*, Vol. 9, p. 293.

day. Contract law governs the relationship between two parties who agree a lawful transaction. Criminal law governs the actions of those who step outside the bounds of what society says is appropriate behaviour towards others and their property. Church law governs the relationships of members of the church to one another and to those outside the church. That's what this book is all about. It is an exploration of the church and the law so that we can better live in relationship with one another and fulfil our mission and calling as a church.

FAQs

Why do I need to learn about the law?

Clergy sometimes say to me: 'I am more interested in mission than in structures and law.' My response is always the same: 'You are part of a law-based church. You agreed to that, both at your ordination and at the time of each appointment. If you are serious about mission, why would you want to waste your time repeating anything other than mission?' I know so many clergy and PCCs who plan some parish project or another, only to discover that they have to start again when they find the legal boundaries prevent them from doing what they had planned. If they had taken the trouble to know a little church law to start with they would not have wasted their valuable mission time by having to do the administrative and legal work twice. The same is true of anyone with responsibility in the church. If we are serious about mission in the Church of England we need to know the rules of the organization we swore to uphold, so that we can work within their boundaries as easily as possible and not waste our time making mistakes which could have been avoided.

Why do we have to be so legalistic?

I would be the first to admit that knowing and obeying the law is just one part of being professional as clergy. But the law is there and we need to take it seriously. The *Guidelines for the Professional Conduct of Clergy* state: 'The clergy should know how church law shapes their exercise of office and ministry, and should respect such regulations as are put in place by the Church.'[7] Others need to know about the law too: churchwardens, readers, PCC members and so on, all need to have an awareness of how church law works to frame the mission and ministry to which they are called. This is not legalism. Legalism is the blind creation of and obedience to laws. This is mission-shaped lawfulness!

How does the church get different types of law?

In the Church of England law can be made in several ways. The most significant laws are passed by General Synod in the form of measures. A measure is sent by Synod to Parliament for scrutiny and then receives the Royal Assent. Measures have the same effect and authority as Acts of Parliament. Measures can apply to anyone affected by their particular subject matter, whether they are members of the church or not. Other forms of legislation include canons – which also receive the Royal Assent and are applicable to those who swear to obey them – schemes, orders and other instruments, which generally have the same force as parliamentary Statutory Instruments. The doctrinal and liturgical documents also have the effect of being church laws and the Thirty Nine Articles, Book of Common Prayer and *Common Worship* services contain rules and directions (often called rubrics) which must be followed.

There is another body of rules which hold a different status from these primary laws. Norman Doe calls this quasi-legislation.[8] This category includes regulations, codes of practice, circulars and guidelines issued either by the central church or by diocesan authorities. These do not have the same authority as measures and canons. Each piece of quasi-legislation should be viewed separately and the enforceability of most has never been tested, but it is generally assumed that most of this legislation would be enforceable and, therefore, should be obeyed. All of this church law sits within the historic common law of the Church of

7 *Guidelines for the Professional Conduct of Clergy*, s. 8.2.
8 Doe, *The Legal Framework of the Church of England*, pp. 16–22.

England known as the *jus commune*. This consists of the laws and customs of the church pre-dating the specific canon law and ecclesiastical law of the modern church.

To *whom does the law apply?*

The answer to this varies according to the type of law. The canons of the Church of England primarily bind those who swear to be bound by them! That, you may think, does not take us very far, but it is tied in to the fact that the Church of England is fundamentally not a 'membership' church. Clergy and readers take an oath agreeing to obey the canons. Churchwardens are bound by the canons which refer to them. Deaconesses and licensed lay workers are bound by the canons which apply to them. Some measures specify who they apply to: for example, if someone is fulfilling a specific role – perhaps during the appointment process – then they will follow these rules. Public law which applies to the church applies to us all anyway. The bottom line is that bishops, archdeacons, clergy, readers, churchwardens, PCCs and Synod members all need to have some understanding of church law and its application. And, I suspect, many more people besides.

Who *enforces the law?*

There are various legal officers in a diocese. Each diocese has a chancellor,[9] appointed by the bishop, who is the judge of the diocesan court known as the Consistory Court. The chancellor is often a barrister. Although the chancellors' jurisdiction used to be wide, today they primarily oversee the faculty jurisdiction of the church. There is an appeal system in each province from a Consistory Court and that is usually to the Court of the Arches (in the Province of Canterbury, presided over by the Dean of Arches) and the Chancery Court (in the Province of York, presided over by the Auditor). In practice the Dean of Arches and the Auditor is the same person.[10] In cases regarding doctrine, ritual or ceremonial

---

9 Ecclesiastical Jurisdiction Measure, 1963, s2.
10 Ecclesiastical Jurisdiction Measure, 1963, s3.

the Court of Ecclesiastical Causes Reserved has jurisdiction. This can serve as the court of first instance if the matter related to an offence by clergy involving a matter of doctrine, ritual or ceremonial. The court also has appellate jurisdiction from a diocesan consistory court where a chancellor certifies that a faculty application involves an issue involving a matter of doctrine, ritual or ceremonial.[11]

Each diocese and each province also has a registrar,[12] often a solicitor, and that person is also the bishop's (or in the case of a Provincial Court, the archbishop's) legal adviser. The registrar does not technically have many legal powers, but his or her role is crucial in the legal administration of the Church of England. The registrar gives legal advice and is often the first point of contact in contentious legal matters.

The archdeacon also has a legal role. Archdeacon's visitations have a legal aspect to them and archdeacons have various legal functions, for example under the Faculty Jurisdiction Measure and the Clergy Discipline Measure.[13] An archdeacon is often the first person that a minister or churchwarden will consult on a legal matter, and most archdeacons have a great deal of experience in such matters and can offer useful advice.

The bishop of a diocese also has a legal role in certain matters, under either specific measures or the canons. This can be a cause of concern and frustration to bishops and their flock alike. Legislation increasingly suggests that one matter or another must be passed to the bishop for a decision. The current debate on the nature of episcopal ministry, which is part of the discussion about the possible ordination of women as bishops, has highlighted this frustration. Many bishops and clergy want to operate a pastoral model of *episcope*, and yet the bishop is increasingly forced to be a legal and administrative adjudicator. After all, he is the senior minister of the diocese. The tension is clear for all to see, and most bishops somehow find their way through this complex role issue.

---

11 Ecclesiastical Jurisdiction Measure, 1963, s10.

12 Ecclesiastical Judges and Legal Officers Measure, 1976, s4.

13 See Chapters 10 and 14 respectively.

What happens when ...

... I don't learn the law?

Just as in the public law of the land, so too in church law, some-times laws come with penalties attached. They are not something we hear much about, but they are there. Let me give you some examples.

The most obvious ones relate to the Clergy Discipline Meas-ure and the Ecclesiastical Jurisdiction Measure. Together these two measures regulate the disciplinary processes of the Church of England. There is power to impose on someone found guilty of an offence or misconduct one of the following penalties: per-manent or limited prohibition (an order preventing a cleric from ministering), removal from office, revocation of a licence, an in-junction or order to do or to refrain from doing a specified act, or a rebuke.[14]

The courts of the Church of England have power to impose financial orders and costs on clergy and others with responsibil-ity in the parish. In fact as recently as 2007 a chancellor ordered a clergyman who wrongly gave permission for a memorial stone to be put into a churchyard to pay a part of the costs of the pro-ceedings which followed. The chancellor did so on the grounds that the clergyman's 'knowledge and application of the (Church-yard) Directions fell well short of what is expected of clergy of the Church of England'.[15] Let this be a warning to us all.

Some public law which applies to the Church of England comes with penalties. For example, the Data Protection Act 1998 per-mits a fine of up to £500 for offences under that Act. There is even power under the Marriage Act 1949 to send someone to prison for up to 14 years for wrongly performing a marriage ceremony!

Having said all that, there are far better reasons for obeying the law than fear of penalty. Loyalty to the oaths we have taken, obedience to the law for its own sake, and even scriptural injunc-tion come to mind!

---

14 Clergy Discipline Measure 2003, s24. It is broadly similar to that in Ecclesiastical Jurisdiction Measure 1963, s49.

15 In *Re Icklesham Churchyard*, October 2007, Chichester Consistory Court.

Resources you should have at your fingertips

- *The Canons of the Church of England.*
- Your Diocesan Handbook.
- James Behrens, *Practical Church Management.*
- This book!

Useful links

- The Church of England web-site has a useful legal section at www.cofe.anglican.org/about/churchlawlegis

- The Canons of the Church of England can be downloaded in pdf format from www.cofe.anglican.org/about/churchlawlegis/canons

- Guidelines for the Professional Conduct of Clergy can be downloaded from www.cofe.anglican.org/lifeevents/ministry/profcond.pdf

- Your diocesan web-site, or someone else's, can be helpful. In my opinion Chichester, Oxford and London diocesan web-sites are particularly good on legal matters. If you have a particular issue, use your favourite search engine and see what you can find.

- The Ecclesiastical Law Society has a web-site at www.ecclawsoc.org.uk

- All Acts of Parliament and Church of England measures can be seen at www.statutelaw.gov.uk/Home.aspx. Just beware to check on the page which first gives you the measure you are looking for, that it is up to date and fully amended. It will tell you if it is not.

3

Churchwardens

A possible scenario

You are fortunate in your parish as you have a fine churchwarden who has done the job for the last eight years and is willing to continue. Her only conditions are that she does not have time to do 'all that paperwork' and she is on holiday when the archdeacon is planning the visitation service. Do either of these things matter?

What you need to know

Who can be a churchwarden

The churchwardens of parishes are chosen in accordance with the Churchwardens Measure 2001.[1] They must be chosen annually not later than 30 April.[2] They must be lay people who are baptized and whose names are on the church electoral roll of the parish, who are actual communicants,[3] who are over 21, and who are not disqualified.[4] They are chosen at the Annual Meeting of Parishioners.[5] Candidates for election at the meeting must be nominated and seconded in writing by someone entitled to attend the meeting. Each nomination paper must include a statement, signed by the person nominated, that they are willing to serve as a churchwarden and are not disqualified. A nomination

---

1 Canon E1(1).

2 Churchwardens Measure 2001, s4.

3 See Church Representation Rules, rule 54 for a definition of this.

4 Churchwardens Measure 2001, s1 – for disqualifications see s2 of the Measure.

5 Churchwardens Measure 2001, s5.

is not valid unless received by the minister of the parish before the commencement of the meeting.[6]

Annual Meeting of Parishioners

A meeting of parishioners must be called each year before 30 April.[7] This is known as the Annual Meeting of Parishioners (AMP – some people still refer to it by its historic name of the Vestry Meeting). This is a joint meeting of anyone whose name is on the church electoral roll of the parish or who is resident in the parish. Residence in this case means someone who has their name on the register of local government electors.[8] The meeting must be called by the minister, or in a vacancy, by the church-wardens.[9] The only usual business of the meeting is the election of churchwardens.

A notice of the meeting must be displayed on or near to the principal door of the parish church for a period including the last two Sundays before the meeting.[10] This is not the same notice as that which is needed for the Annual Parochial Church Meeting (APCM, see Chapter 4), even if the two meetings are held on the same day.

The minister is the chairman of the meeting, and if there is a vacancy a chairman is chosen by the meeting.[11] Voting is conducted in the same way as at an APCM.[12] Clergy who are resident in the parish are entitled to vote at the AMP, but the minister (that is, the incumbent or priest in charge) is not. If the AMP is to be on the same evening as the APCM it is wise to hold the AMP before the APCM. This allows anyone nominated as churchwarden, but not elected, to stand for election to the PCC if they so desire.

---

6 Churchwardens Measure 2001, s4(4).
7 Churchwardens Measure 2001, s4.
8 Churchwardens Measure 2001, s5(1).
9 Churchwardens Measure 2001, s4(2).
10 Churchwardens Measure 2001, s4(4).
11 Churchwardens Measure 2001, s4(5).
12 Church Representation Rules, rules 13 and 11.

The role of churchwardens

The churchwardens are officers of the bishop.[13] Not later than 31 July in each year, each person chosen for the office of church-warden must appear before the bishop, or his substitute, and be admitted to office. Before admission they must make a declar-ation that they will faithfully and diligently perform the duties of office and also that they are not disqualified.[14] It is common for this admission to be conducted by the archdeacon at his or her annual visitation service.

Churchwardens should be people who will actively represent the laity and will co-operate with the incumbent. They should use their best endeavours to encourage the parishioners in the practice of their faith and to promote unity and peace among them. They are to maintain order and decency in the church and churchyard, especially during the time of divine service.[15] Many of the historic duties that belonged to the churchwardens are now the responsibility of the PCC. However, there are still some specific responsibilities that belong to the churchwardens.

The churchwardens, with the advice and direction of the min-ister, are responsible for providing the bread and wine for com-munion.[16] This responsibility is usually funded by the PCC.

It is the duty of the churchwardens (and the minister), if any alterations, additions, removals, or repairs are proposed to be made in the fabric, ornaments, or furniture of the church, to obtain the faculty before proceeding with the work.[17]

Terrier, Inventory and Log Book

These three documents are a vital part of a churchwarden's work, as they relate to the tasks that are specific to the churchwarden's role, rather than to the PCC generally. It is the duty of the church-wardens to compile and maintain a full list of all lands (called a

---

13 Canon E1(4).
14 Canon E1(2)(a).
15 Canon E1(4).
16 Canon B17(1).
17 Canon F13(3), see Chapter 14.

Terrier) and a full list of all articles (called an Inventory) belonging to the church. It is also a duty to keep a Log Book and note in it all alterations, additions and repairs to, and other events affecting the church and the lands and articles belonging to the parish and of the location of any other documents relating to these matters. In carrying out this duty the churchwardens act in consultation with the minister.[18] Usually these documents are inherited from the outgoing churchwardens, so unless something has gone wrong the current churchwardens usually only need to keep them up to date.

It is the duty of the churchwardens at least once in each year to inspect, or cause an inspection to be made of, the fabric of the church and all articles belonging to the church. They must deliver to the PCC and then to the APCM a report on the fabric of the church and all articles belonging to the church (referred to as 'the annual fabric report'). This should include an account of all steps taken or proposed during the previous year for their protection and maintenance and, in particular, for the implementation of any recommendation contained in a quinquennial report. The annual fabric report must be delivered to the PCC at its last meeting before the APCM.[19]

The legal ownership of the plate, ornaments, and other movable goods of the church is vested in the churchwardens during their time of office. The Inventory is not, therefore, just a cumbersome list of items the church owns. When their successors are sworn into office they become the legal owners of the same items, and it is important for everyone's protection that the process of passing on ownership from one churchwarden to the next is taken seriously. On going out of office the churchwardens should deliver to their successors any goods of the church remaining in their possession together with the Inventory, which must be checked by their successors.[20]

---

18 Care of Churches and Ecclesiastical Jurisdiction Measure 1991, s4.

19 Care of Churches and Ecclesiastical Jurisdiction Measure 1991, s5.

20 Canon E1(5).

Length of service

A person is disqualified from being chosen for the office of churchwarden when they have served as a churchwarden of the same parish for six successive periods of office. The person must then take a two-year break before they are eligible again.[21]

A Meeting of Parishioners may, by resolution, decide that this provision shall not apply in relation to the parish concerned. Any such resolution may be revoked by a subsequent Meeting of Parishioners.[22] Such a resolution could be considered by a (properly called) 'Special' Meeting of Parishioners – it does not have to be done at the Annual Meeting of Parishioners. The resolution has immediate effect. So a 'Special' Meeting of Parishioners could be held (in, say, March) to consider a resolution to set aside the automatic disqualification. If it did pass such a resolution, that would then be effective at the forthcoming AMP (to be held in, say, April). The same resolution could be considered at the AMP, immediately before the election of churchwardens is conducted – but with the disadvantage that (because the meeting has begun) no additional nominations are possible at that point.

PCC membership

Churchwardens take up their office and legal responsibilities at the time of their admission, not their election. Oddly, however, they are *ex officio* members of the PCC from the date of their election. Outgoing churchwardens, assuming for a moment that they are different people, remain members of the PCC until their successors are admitted, as they are still wardens until then. It will not be unusual, therefore, for four churchwardens to be eligible to attend the first PCC meeting following the APCM.

---

21 Churchwardens Measure 2001, s3.
22 Churchwardens Measure 2001, s3.

FAQs

What are the people's warden and vicar's warden?

It used to be the custom that these two titles were used in parishes, but this has long since gone. No such distinction now exists.

Can a parish have deputy churchwardens?

There is only one place in the Church Representation Rules where deputy churchwardens are mentioned – that is in Rule 18, which is specifically about parishes with more than one church. In addition a team ministry may have deputy churchwardens, elected in each district of the team. The details of how this is to be done should be in the scheme establishing the team ministry or in a document known as a 'bishop's instrument under hand', attached to it. If in doubt ask your diocesan registry for a copy of the relevant pastoral scheme.[23]

However, there is no reason why a parish cannot have assistant churchwardens or senior sidemen (the term 'deputy churchwardens' is best avoided for clarity). These titles could describe someone who assists the churchwardens in fulfilling their role. Indeed the role of sidesmen is described as 'to promote the cause of true religion in the parish and to assist the churchwardens in the discharge of their duties'.[24] A useful by-product of such roles is that they make the workload manageable and train up people ready to take on the full role in due time.

How can a churchwarden resign?

A person may resign the office of churchwarden by giving written notice of intention to resign to the bishop by post. The resignation takes effect and the office is formally vacated two months after service of the notice or on an earlier date determined by the bishop.[25] The office of churchwarden is automatically vacated if

---

23 There are still a few parishes where the appointment of deputy wardens is based on ancient custom.

24 Canon E2.

25 Churchwardens Measure 2001, s7.

the name of the person concerned is removed from the church electoral roll of the parish under rule 1 of the Church Representation Rules or the churchwarden becomes disqualified under section 2 of the measure.[26]

When does a churchwarden's term of office end?

Churchwardens are elected and admitted for a term of one year. If they are re-elected they continue in office by virtue of being admitted the following year, so it is important to attend the admission service each year, even if a churchwarden has served in the previous year. If a successor is elected, the previous churchwarden continues in office until the new churchwarden is admitted. If no successor is elected and admitted, the previous churchwarden continues in office until 31 July, on which date their term in office concludes. Again this is important as the churchwardens have vested in them, during their term of office, the property in the plate, ornaments, and other movable goods of the church. It is not, therefore, simply a matter of convenience as to whether a churchwarden is properly in office, but a matter of property law.

What happens when ...

... a minister does not agree to the election of a warden?

Churchwardens are elected by the Meeting of Parishioners as their representatives. It is not, therefore, generally for the minister to decide who is to be a churchwarden, or to unduly influence the nominations or elections. However, there may be rare occasions when a minister is not comfortable with the written nominations received prior to the AMP, and there are specific provisions to direct what may or may not be done in such circumstances.

It may occasionally appear to the minister of the parish that the election of a particular person would give rise to serious difficulties between the minister and that person in the carrying out

---

26 Churchwardens Measure 2001, s8.

of their respective functions. It is then open to the minister, after the close of nominations but before the election is conducted, to make a statement to the effect that only one churchwarden is to be elected by the meeting. In that event one churchwarden is appointed by the minister from among the nominations. The name of the person so appointed is announced before the election is conducted, and the other churchwarden will then be elected by the meeting.[27]

It should be noted that the minister can only choose a churchwarden from among those duly nominated. The minister cannot stop the person who caused the concern from subsequently being elected by the meeting. The minister does not have to state who it is, from among the nominated candidates, that has caused him or her to exercise this right under the measure. Indeed, for pastoral reasons it seems unwise to do so. It may also be defamatory if you are not very careful!

... an elected warden is not admitted to office?

If an elected warden does not attend the admission service then they do not become churchwarden for the year, despite being elected. In this situation a casual vacancy arises and the process for filling it must be followed.[28] The vacancy occurs on 31 July after the Annual Meeting of Parishioners. Up to that time the previous churchwarden remains in office, be it the same individual or someone else.

... there is a casual vacancy?

A casual vacancy can be filled at any time after a churchwarden resigns or ceases to hold office. A Meeting of Parishioners must be called, using the same notice and process as for the Annual Meeting of Parishioners.[29]

---

27 Churchwardens Measure 2001, s4.5.
28 Churchwardens Measure 2001, s1.
29 Churchwardens Measure 2001, s4(8).

... we can't find any churchwardens?

In small parishes, particularly, there may be times when no one can be found to be churchwarden. In law this problem is not addressed. The law simply states that there shall be churchwardens. This emphasizes the need to try every possible means to ensure that the situation does not arise. If, however, it does occur then the outgoing churchwarden will remain in post until 31 July and their term of office will then end. It is suggested that it would be good practice for the minister (and any continuing churchwarden) to sign off the Terrier and Inventory so as to protect the outgoing churchwarden.

Resources you should have at your fingertips

- Churchwardens Measure 2001.

- Canon E1.

- Terrier, Inventory and Log Books: it is possible to buy printed versions of these three documents which make the keeping of these records very straightforward. From time to time it may be wise or necessary to completely renew these documents. They are available from church bookshops. If a new Terrier, Inventory or Log Book is started the old one should be kept carefully in the parish or passed to the diocesan archive.

Useful links

- Forms for calling a meeting to elect churchwardens, nomination forms and notice of election forms are available from several diocesan web-sites; see for example,
www.southwark.anglican.org/download/apcm/index.htm
www.leicester.anglican.org/APCM/index.html#downloads
www.diochi.org.uk/resources/apcm/index.htm

- There are a number of handbooks which may be of use to churchwardens. These include:

- Martin Dudley and Virginia Rounding, *Churchwardens: A Survival Guide*, London, SPCK, 2003.

- Kenneth M. Macmorran and Timothy Briden, *Handbook for Churchwardens and Parochial Church Councillors*, London, Continuum, 2007.

- Graham Jeffery, *The Churchwarden's Year: Church Maintenance Calendar*, London, Church House Publishing, 1994.

- John Pitchford, *ABC for the PCC: A Handbook for Church Council Members*, London, Continuum, 2008

- *The Churchwarden's Yearbook* is a diary specifically marketed towards churchwardens and contains lots of useful information.

4

APCMs

A possible scenario

It is the middle of January and Ash Wednesday is approaching. Easter is early this year and the parish always has its annual meeting before Palm Sunday. Fortunately the churchwarden tells you that you do not need to worry about the shortage of time – this is not a 'renewal year' so you don't need to do much! What does he mean, and is he right?

What you need to know

As the time for an Annual Parochial Church Meeting approaches it is wise to read this chapter, together with Chapters 3 and 5, so as to get the full picture of what must be done.

Electoral roll

In every parish there must be an electoral roll.[1] The roll is kept by an Electoral Roll Officer, appointed by the PCC.[2] A lay person is entitled to have their name entered on the roll of a parish if they are baptized, sixteen years old or more, and have signed an application form for enrolment and a declaration that they are either:

- a member of the Church of England or of a church in communion with the Church of England[3] and are resident in the parish; or

---

1 Church Representation Rules, rule 1(1).
2 Church Representation Rules, Appx II, 1(f).
3 For a definition of this see Chapter 21.

- a non-resident member of the Church of England who has habitually attended public worship in the parish during a period of six months prior to enrolment; or
- a member in good standing of a church which subscribes to the doctrine of the Holy Trinity (not being a church in communion with the Church of England) and they are prepared to declare themselves to be a member of the Church of England having habitually attended public worship in the parish during a period of six months prior to enrolment.[4]

The roll should record, as a minimum for each person enrolled, their name and address,[5] and date of enrolment,[6] and date of birth for any under age 16[7] until they reach that age. It may be helpful to add telephone numbers and email addresses.[8] It would be sensible to maintain a complete record of dates of enrolment and removal for all persons who are or have been on the roll (and retain the evidence justifying a removal).[9]

Each year the roll is formally revised prior to the APCM. Every sixth year the roll is completely renewed. Full details are set out in the Church Representation Rules (CRR).[10] The PCC Electoral Roll Officer may add or remove names from the roll under certain circumstances between revisions.[11]

Annual Parochial Church Meeting

In every parish, not later than 30 April, there must be an Annual Parochial Church Meeting (usually referred to as the APCM).[12] All lay people whose names are on the roll of the parish and all clergy licensed to the parish are entitled to attend the meeting and to take part in its proceedings.[13] The APCM is to be convened by

---

4 Church Representation Rules, rule 1(2).
5 Church Representation Rules, rule 1(11).
6 Church Representation Rules, rule 10(1)(a).
7 Church Representation Rules, rule 1(2).
8 Church Representation Rules, Appx II, para 4(b).
9 See Chapter 19 for information on Data Protection Act 1998.
10 Church Representation Rules, rule 2.
11 Church Representation Rules, rule 1(9).
12 Church Representation Rules, rule 6(1).
13 Church Representation Rules, rule 6(2).

the minister of the parish. A notice must be put on or near to the principal door of every church in the parish, and every building licensed for public worship in the parish, for a period including the last two Sundays before the day of the meeting.[14]

The date, time and place of the meeting shall be decided by the previous APCM, or by the PCC (which may overrule any direction given by a previous APCM) or in the absence of any such direction from the APCM or PCC it is decided by the minister.[15] It should be noted that the APCM is not the same as the Annual Meeting of Parishioners referred to in Chapter 3, although they are usually held on the same day. The two meetings must be convened separately and distinguished from each other at the time.

It is important to make proper preparations for the APCM and there is a detailed timetable which must be followed. The APCM must take place no later than 30 April, so plan ahead. More time is required in a year when the roll is renewed rather than revised. The next such years are 2013, 2019, etc. Set a provisional date for the APCM and follow the timetable in the table opposite. If the dates will not work, try again with a later APCM date (but still before 30 April). Prior to an APCM the PCC must receive and approve the churchwardens' fabric report[16] and the treasurer's accounts and financial report.[17]

The chairman of the APCM is usually the minister of the parish, or if he or she is not present the vice-chairman of the PCC.[18] Voting at the meeting is usually by show of hands but there are other possibilities (see below).[19] In the case of an equal division of votes, the chairman of the meeting has a casting vote unless the chairman is ordained and the vote is for the election of the laity representatives. In that case, if there is an equal vote the result is to be decided by drawing lots.[20]

---

14 Church Representation Rules, rule 7(1).
15 Church Representation Rules, rule 7(2).
16 See Chapter 3.
17 See Chapters 5 and 16.
18 Church Representation Rules, rule 8.
19 Church Representation Rules, rule 11.
20 Church Representation Rules, rule 8.

A	In 2013, 2019, etc. A NEW ROLL IS PREPARED	CRR Ref
Time before APCM	**Action**	
At least 2 months before APCM	Not less than 2 months before APCM, publish the notice that a new roll is being prepared. Notice remains up for 14+ days. Start preparing new roll. At every service on the next 2 Sundays inform congregation of preparation of new roll.	2.4
	PCC must take reasonable steps to inform all previous roll members, explaining that fresh enrolment is required this year. An early article in parish magazine could be useful here. Those whose names could legitimately be removed from the old roll under CRR 1.9 need not be contacted.	2.5
15–28 days before APCM	The new roll is completed not less than 15 or more than 28 days before APCM.	2.6
At least 14 days before APCM	The new roll is published for 14+ days before APCM (it comes into effect on publication, and the previous roll lapses). No names can be added to or removed from the roll between now and end of APCM, except any errors or omissions rectified, see CRR 2.7; and CRR 1.2 adding any qualifying U16s on their birthday.	2.7 1.2
	Continue at section C	

B	In intermediate years – THE ROLL IS REVISED	
At least 30 days before APCM	Publish notice of revision of the roll. (It is inadvisable for this to be done before 1 January.) Thirty days is the absolute legal minimum required and assumes a revision period of only one day. I suggest that 6 weeks, with a revision period of 15 days including three Sundays makes more sense of the process.	2.1
	Allow 14+ days gap after the notice goes up	2.1
At least 16 days before APCM	Revision commences. (The rules do not say how long the revision should take; I commonly allow 15 days, which includes 3 Sundays, but it need not be so. It could be as little as one day.)	2.1
	During revision period, review all enrolments or removals since last year; make new enrolments and removals.	2.2
15–28 days before APCM	Revision completed, revision period closes (not less than 15 or more than 28 days before APCM).	2.1
At least 14 days before APCM	Revised roll is published for not less than 14 days before APCM; together with list of names removed since last year. No names can be added or removed between now and end of APCM, except any errors or omissions rectified, see CRR 2.3; and CRR 1.2 adding any qualifying U16s on their birthday.	2.3 1.2

C	In all years, after [A] or [B]	
*At least 2 Sundays before APCM	*Publish notice of APCM for period to include the last 2 Sundays before the APCM (but could helpfully include 3 or 4 Sundays).	7.1*
*At least 7 days before APCM	*Display PCC financial statements (already audited/independently examined, and approved and signed at a PCC meeting).	9.3*
	APCM is not later than 30 April	6.1
After the APCM	Send copy of financial statements and reports as approved by APCM to the diocese within 28 days. (Although now no longer mandatory under CRR 9.4, it remains good practice to publish and display these reports and statements.)	9.4
	Publish results of elections, for 14+ days. Notify secretaries of deanery synod and diocesan synod.	11.9 11.10
Not later than 1 June	Notify roll numbers to secretary of the diocesan synod and publish copy notice on or near church door for 14+ days.	4

* These two items could therefore precede the publishing of the new or revised roll.[21]

---

21 My thanks to Archdeacon Peter Taylor for this table.

Agenda

The APCM must receive from the PCC and is free to discuss:

1 A report on changes in the roll since the last APCM or, in a year in which a new roll is prepared, a report on the numbers entered on the new roll.

2 An annual report on the proceedings of the PCC and the activities of the parish generally, usually prepared by the PCC Secretary.

3 The financial report and accounts of the PCC for the year ending on 31 December immediately preceding the meeting, independently examined or audited according to the size of the turnover.[22]

4 A report upon the fabric, goods and ornaments of the church or churches of the parish from the churchwardens.[23]

5 A report on the proceedings of the deanery synod.[24]

The APCM also elects or appoints the following people:

6 Elect in every third year parochial representatives of the laity to the deanery synod.

7 Elect parochial representatives of the laity to the PCC.[25]

8 Appoint sidesmen.

9 Appoint an independent examiner or auditor to the council for the following year who must not be a member of the council.

And finally:

10 Any person entitled to attend the APCM may ask any question about parochial church matters, or bring about a discussion of any matter of parochial or general church interest, by moving a general resolution or by moving to give any particular recommendation to the council in relation to its

---

22 See Chapter 16.
23 Care of Churches and Ecclesiastical Jurisdiction Measure 1991, s5.
24 Church Representation Rules, rule 9(1).
25 See Chapter 5.

duties.[26] It is worth noting that under this last provision the APCM cannot pass a resolution directing the PCC to take any particular action, although it may pass a resolution recommending a certain course of action. The PCC must always retain its responsibilities for deciding on matters relating to its powers,[27] although it will be obliged to take into consideration a resolution passed by the APCM.[28]

The elections and appointments must be carried out in the order set out at numbers 6–9 above. In effect these ten items are, therefore, a standard agenda for an APCM.

FAQs

What must be displayed publicly before the APCM?

You will need to display before the APCM:

- Notice of the APCM.
- The financial report and accounts following approval by the PCC.
- The revised or renewed electoral roll

Details of the timings are in the table above. These things are in addition to similar documents for the Annual Meeting of Parishioners.[29]

What needs to go into the annual report?

The annual report is a sizeable document which contains reports and accounts. Items 1–5 in the agenda (above) should be included together with a variety of information required under the Charities Act 1993. The APCM is effectively the annual meeting of a charitable trust and must be conducted with care and attention

---

26 Church Representation Rules, rule 9.
27 See Chapter 5.
28 Parochial Church Councils (Powers) Measure 1956, s2(3).
29 See Chapter 3.

to detail. For further information on the financial elements of the report see elsewhere.[30]

Why do we need to have two meetings?

The Annual Meeting of Parishioners is open to anyone who either lives in the parish or is on the electoral roll. The APCM is only open to those who are on the electoral roll and to certain defined clergy.[31] In theory, therefore, it is necessary, even if the meetings are on the same day, to pause and 'cast out the general public' before the APCM begins. In practice it is likely that the attendance at both meetings (if they are held on the same day) will be the same, but you need to be aware of the distinction, especially at the point where any vote is taken.

How should votes be conducted at the APCM?

Voting at an APCM can be by show of hands or by paper vote. The chairman of the meeting has a second (or casting) vote unless it is in an election for a lay representative, in which case a clerical chairman would not. In that case the result should be determined by drawing lots.[32]

Can someone have a postal vote for an APCM?

Yes. A previous APCM would have to decide to allow this method by a two-thirds majority, and it would mean that results of elections have to be deferred until after the postal vote has taken place. Since nominations can be taken at the meeting, any postal voting cannot take place until after the meeting. This means that voting at the meeting would have to be by paper vote, and the voting papers would be kept and counted only when postal votes have also been returned. Announcement of any election results would thus be delayed to a later date. The rules also allow single transferable voting.[33]

---

30 See Chapter 16.
31 See Church Representation Rules, rule 6(3).
32 Church Representation Rules, rule 11.
33 Church Representation Rules, rule 12.

Who may be removed from the electoral roll and when?

It is the duty of the parish electoral roll officer to keep the roll constantly up to date by the addition and removal of names and to report such additions and removals at the next meeting of the PCC. The grounds on which a removal may happen are set out in the rules. There are three straightforward grounds: if a person has died, or becomes a clerk in Holy Orders, or requests in writing that his or her name be removed. There are three further grounds which may need the electoral roll officer to take care. If a person ceases to reside in the parish their name may be removed unless they continue habitually to attend public worship in the parish. If a person has not been resident in the parish and has not habitually attended public worship in the parish during the preceding six months their name may be removed. Both these last two grounds have an exception attached to them. If a person has been prevented from attending by virtue of illness or other sufficient cause then their name should remain on the roll. This is a judgement which the officer should consider carefully. The last ground is that the person was not entitled to have his or her name entered on the roll at the time when it was entered.[34] Again caution is advised. There is a full discussion of this issue in an article by David Lamming in the *Ecclesiastical Law Journal*.[35]

What happens when ...

... the meeting has finished?

After the APCM the PCC Secretary needs to display a notice of the results of elections. (There is a similar requirement relating to the election of churchwardens at the Annual Meeting of Parishioners.[36]) They should notify the Diocesan Secretary of the number on the roll.[37] They must send the annual report and

---

34 Church Representation Rules, rule 1(9).

35 D. Lamming, 'The Church Electoral Roll', *Ecclesiastical Law Journal*, 8 (2006), p. 438.

36 See Chapter 3.

37 Church Representation Rules, rule 4.

financial statement to the Diocesan Secretary.[38] They should also notify both the Diocesan Secretary and the Deanery Secretary of the results of any elections to the deanery synod.

Resources you should have at your fingertips

It is vital to have the current version of Church Representation Rules. It is updated every few years, so it is always worth checking with your local bookshop, or on-line, that you have the latest edition in your hands. This vital document which should be in the hands of every clergyperson in the Church of England is, bizarrely, not available as an on-line document.

Useful links

- The forms to be used for all the notices at an APCM are in the Church Representation Rules. There are a number of diocesan web-sites which have on line versions which could be edited and saved to your computer, thus saving work in following years:
www.southwark.anglican.org/download/apcm/index.htm
www.leicester.anglican.org/APCM/index.html#downloads
www.diochi.org.uk/resources/apcm/index.htm

- These sites also have examples of nomination papers. These are not set out in the legislation, but the versions on-line may be helpful as examples of good practice to adapt to your local situation.

- The full details of what is required in an annual report are set out in *The Charities Act and the PCC* (3rd edition) which can be downloaded from www.cofe.anglican.org/info/finance/charitiesact.pdf and see Chapter 16.

---

38 Church Representation Rules, rule 9(4).

5

PCCs

A possible scenario

The reader in your new parish chairs the PCC and wishes to continue doing so after your arrival. After all, he has been a member of the PCC for 40 years and will obviously be more in touch with the members. Do you object, and on what grounds?

What you need to know

Membership of the PCC

Every parish in the Church of England must have a Parochial Church Council (PCC). The PCC of a parish consists of:[1]

- all clerks in Holy Orders beneficed in or licensed to the parish;
- any deaconess or lay worker licensed to the parish;[2]
- in the case of a team ministry, all the members of the team;
- the churchwardens;[3]
- such readers of the parish as the APCM may determine;
- anyone whose names are on the roll of the parish and who are lay members of any deanery synod, diocesan synod or the General Synod;
- elected lay representatives;
- co-opted members, if the PCC so decides, not exceeding in number one-fifth of the representatives of the elected laity or two persons, whichever is the greater.

---

1 Church Representation Rules, rule 14(1).

2 This does not mean a lay person employed by the parish, but simply a person who holds the bishop's licence.

3 See the note on churchwardens and the PCC in Chapter 3.

Ex officio members

The representatives elected to the deanery synod or diocesan synod hold *ex officio* membership for the period of that synod's triennium and any member of the parish who is on General Synod holds *ex officio* membership for the period of that synod's quinquennium. Their term of membership on the PCC, therefore, usually ends when their time on synod ends. There is nothing to prevent them standing for election to PCC even though they are already *ex officio*. This has the advantage that their membership of the PCC would continue, although on the other hand such an election would block a place from being available to someone else.

To illustrate some of the issues here let me describe a large parish I have recently served in. The full-time youth worker is paid by the diocese but is not on the PCC *ex officio* as she is not licensed. She is eligible for election to the PCC. There have been up to four readers, and the APCM has power to decide which of them should be on the PCC. There is a retired self-supporting minister who works full time and is fully part of the clergy team. She has PTO (permission to officiate) from the bishop. She is not *ex officio* but could be co-opted. A part-time chaplain at the local hospital gives support in the parish and is treated as part of the clergy team. Her licence is to the hospital. She is licensed in the parish but not to the parish, so she too would not be *ex officio* on the PCC, but could be co-opted. There is a Church Army sister. She is licensed to the parish and would be on the PCC as a result. There are two other clergy, both stipendiary, one as associate vicar and the other as curate. Both are on the PCC by virtue of their licence. And then there's me. I give only 5 per cent of my time to the work (the rest being the diocesan Continuing Ministerial Education (CME) adviser), but hold a licence to the parish, so despite being less of a team member than some of the others I am *ex officio* on the PCC. There are eight churchwardens, but only two of them are elected to be parish churchwardens, and those two are on the PCC, the others (who are technically assistant churchwardens) need to stand for election.

Numbers of elected lay representatives

Having unscrambled who is *ex officio* (and it is unlikely to be as complicated in most places), it is necessary next to decide the number of lay members to be elected. This is set out in the table below.

Number on electoral roll	Number of representatives
0–49	6
50–99	9
100–199	12
200 or more	15 This is the maximum number.

Note: These figures represent the number of elected representatives, not the total size of the PCC which may be significantly higher.[4]

There is provision for the number of members to be changed from those in this table. The number of elected representatives may be changed by a resolution passed at any APCM, which will take effect at the next APCM.[5] In order to work with a body whose size is appropriate to the local setting and representative of the parish it may well be appropriate for either the PCC or the standing committee to propose alternative figures to the APCM for it to consider. Unless such a resolution is passed the figures in the table apply.

Term of office of elected lay representatives

Lay representatives must normally be elected for a three-year term, with one-third retiring annually in rotation.[6] If this has not been the practice then in the first year when this pattern is used

---

4 Church Representation Rules, rule 14(1)(g).
5 Church Representation Rules, rule 14(1)(g).
6 Church Representation Rules, rule 16(1).

all members are to be elected and then their terms of office (one, two and three years) are to be determined by lot. When a casual vacancy occurs it shall be filled for the remainder of the term of the person who ceased to be a member.[7]

The APCM may pass a resolution that every place should be filled by annual election instead of the pattern described in the above paragraph.[8] Such a resolution would seem to take immediate effect. A resolution that all members of the PCC should be elected annually must be reviewed every six years and unless a new resolution is passed the APCM must revert to the normal method.[9]

The APCM may decide that no representative of the laity may hold office for more than a specified number of years continuously and may also decide that after a specified interval a person who has ceased to be eligible by reason of such decision may again stand for election.[10] To be qualified for election, a person must have been on the electoral roll for at least six months prior to the APCM, unless he or she is under 18.[11]

Functions and purpose of PCC

It is the duty of the minister and the PCC to consult together on matters of general concern and importance to the parish. [12] The PCC is a body corporate in its own right; in other words it has a legal status to which attach certain rights and duties.[13] The functions of a PCC include:

1 Co-operation with the minister in promoting in the parish the whole mission of the church, pastoral, evangelistic, social and ecumenical.

---

7 Church Representation Rules, rule 16(2).
8 Church Representation Rules, rule 16(3).
9 Church Representation Rules, rule 16(4).
10 Church Representation Rules, rule 17.
11 Church Representation Rules, rule 10.
12 Parochial Church Councils (Powers) Measure 1956, s2(1).
13 Parochial Church Councils (Powers) Measure 1956, s3.

2 The consideration and discussions of any matters concerning the Church of England or of religious or public interest.

3 Making known and putting into effect any provision made by the diocesan synod or the deanery synod.

4 Giving advice to the diocesan synod and the deanery synod on any matter referred to the council.

5 Raising such matters as the council consider appropriate with the diocesan synod or deanery synod.[14]

A senior Law Lord recently commented:

> The key to the role of the PCC lies in the first of its general functions: co-operation with the minister in promoting in the parish the whole mission of the church. Its other more particular functions are to be seen as ways of carrying out this general function.[15]

Other powers, rights and responsibilities of the PCC include:

1 Responsibility for the financial affairs of the church including the collection and administration of all moneys raised for church purposes and the keeping of accounts.

2 Responsibility for the care, maintenance, preservation and insurance of the fabric of the church and its goods and ornaments.

3 Responsibility for the care and maintenance of any churchyard (open or closed).[16]

4 Power to frame an annual budget for the work of the church in the parish and to take steps to raise money.

5 Power, jointly with the minister, to determine how money will be spent.

---

14 Parochial Church Councils (Powers) Measure 1956, s2(2).

15 *Lord Rodgers of Earlsferry, Aston Cantlow and Wilmcote with Billesley PCC v Wallbank* [2004] 1 AC 546, [2003] 3All ER 1213, HL, at para. 156.

16 1–3 are all under Parochial Church Councils (Powers) Measure 1956, s4.

6 Power to make representations to the bishop on any matter affecting the welfare of the church in the parish.[17]

7 The right to decide, jointly with the incumbent, on the form of service to be used.[18]

8 The right to be consulted before there is a change of vesture in the church.[19]

9 The right to be consulted before the minister decides where Morning and Evening Prayer will be said other than in the parish church.[20]

10 The right to agree with the minister to dispense with the statutory services on an occasional basis or to apply jointly to the bishop to dispense with them on a regular basis.[21]

11 The right to agree to the appointment or dismissal of an organist, choirmaster or director of music.[22]

12 Certain rights and duties under the ecumenical canons.[23]

13 Rights and duties when a vacancy occurs in the benefice.[24]

14 The right to be consulted about pastoral reorganization.[25]

15 The right to receive the Terrier, Inventory and Log Book from the churchwardens for inspection once each year.[26]

16 The right to receive a report from the churchwardens as to the fabric, at the PCC meeting prior to the APCM.[27]

17 Rights and duties relating to the ministry of ordained women in the parish.[28]

---

17 4–6 are all under Parochial Church Councils (Powers) Measure 1956, s7.

18 Canon B3(1).

19 Canon B8(2).

20 Canon B11(2).

21 Canon B14A(1).

22 Canon B20(1).

23 B43 and B44 – see Chapter 17.

24 Patronage (Benefices) Measure 1986, see Chapter 10.

25 Pastoral Measure 1983, s3.

26 Care of Churches and Ecclesiastical Jurisdiction Measure 1991, s5.

27 Care of Churches and Ecclesiastical Jurisdiction Measure 1991, s5.

28 Priests (Ordination of Women) Measure 1993 and the Episcopal Ministry Act of Synod 1993.

18 Rights and duties relating to the financial affairs of the church.[29]

19 Rights and duties relating to property owned by the church.[30]

20 The right to be consulted about the sale of the parsonage house.[31]

21 The right to consent to the extension of tenure of office of a priest beyond the age of 70.[32]

PCC meetings

The Church Representation Rules set out general provisions relating to PCC meetings.[33] These include provisions regarding the officers of the Council, the frequency of meetings, the power to call meetings, notice required for a meeting, chairman of the meetings, quorum, agenda and order of business, place of meetings, voting at meetings, minutes, committees of the PCC and the validity of proceedings.[34]

PCC committees

The only committee which a PCC must have is a standing committee. This must consist of at least five people, and the minister and churchwardens are *ex officio* members. At least two others must be elected by the PCC from among their number.[35] The PCC may appoint any other committees it chooses, and may include in the membership of sub-committees people who are not members of the council.[36]

---

29 See Chapter 16.
30 See Chapter 14.
31 Parsonages Measure 1938, s3.
32 Ecclesiastical Offices (Age Limit) Measure 1975.
33 Church Representation Rules, Appx II.
34 Church Representation Rules, Appx II.
35 Church Representation Rules, Appx II, para. 14.
36 Church Representation Rules, Appx II, para. 15.

FAQs

Who is the chairman of a PCC?

The chairman of the PCC is always the minister of the parish.[37] There must also be an elected vice-chairman of the PCC who must be a lay person.[38] This is not the same as asking who may act as chair for a particular meeting. Think of this as the difference between the role of chairman and the function of chairing a meeting. The role of chairman is always held by the minister. However, the chairman may for any reason decide to vacate the chair for part or all of any meeting. Generally if a minister chooses to do this the chair passes to the vice-chairman. If neither is present the meeting may choose a chairman.[39]

What is the quorum of a PCC?

One-third.[40] It is worth noting that this means one-third of all members (*ex officio*, elected and co-opted), not only of elected members.

How many PCC meetings must we have?

At least four per year.[41] There is no reason why you may not have more.

Who sets the agenda for the PCC?

The Church Representation Rules are not clear about this. They simply say that the secretary must send the agenda to members seven days before the meeting.[42] The secretary has a duty to put

---

37 Church Representation Rules, Appx II, para. 1(a).
38 Church Representation Rules, Appx II, para. 1(b).
39 Church Representation Rules, Appx II para. 5.
40 Church Representation Rules, Appx II, para. 6.
41 Church Representation Rules, Appx II, para. 2.
42 Church Representation Rules, Appx II, para 4.

certain items on the agenda.[43] In my experience it is usual for the secretary to be responsible for ensuring that an agenda is prepared and notice given, but to do so in consultation with the chairman. Business which is not on the agenda can only be discussed if three-quarters of the PCC members present at the meeting agree.[44]

Can a minister stop anyone being elected to the PCC?

So long as someone is qualified to stand for election, the election process for lay representatives is entirely lay and a minister cannot intervene.[45]

What are district church councils and when can we have them?

In a team ministry or in a parish with more than one place of worship it is possible to establish district church councils. In teams they will be set up at the same time as the team and details of their constitution, rights and duties will be in the pastoral scheme. Contact your diocesan registry for a copy if you do not have one. In parishes with more than one place of worship the APCM, with the approval of the bishop's council, may establish district church councils.[46] It is wise to contact your diocesan pastoral secretary for advice at an early stage.

Who owns parish property?

The church and churchyard are vested in the incumbent. However, the nature of that ownership is subject to the faculty jurisdiction of the chancellor, so incumbents can't just do as they please. They generally may not dispose of the property as it is

---

43 Church Representation Rules, Appx II, para 4 (the secretary must put onto the agenda any motion or business duly notified to the secretary by a member of the council).

44 Church Representation Rules, Appx II, para 6.

45 Church Representation Rules, rules 10 and 11.

46 Church Representation Rules, rule 18.

to be passed on to their successors. Care and maintenance of the church and churchyard is the responsibility of the PCC.[47]

The churchwardens have vested in them legal ownership of the plate, ornaments, and other movable goods of the church during their time of office. Again, they have very restricted rights as to what they may do with them.[48]

The parsonage house is owned by the incumbent. The incumbent may not dispose of it without the consent of the parsonages committee of the diocese, the bishop and the Church Commissioners.[49] Upkeep is the responsibility of the diocese.[50]

Other property may be owned by the PCC (such as church halls etc.) but may not be acquired or sold without the consent of the diocesan board of finance.[51]

Can an employee of the PCC be a member?

Once again we find that it is not easy to give a simple answer. The members of a PCC are appointed to promote its charitable purpose, and as such they are in a position analogous to trustees. It has long been held that trustees cannot benefit from the trust. The most obvious examples of such an issue would be the parish administrator or youth worker who is an employee of the PCC. The best advice seems to be that they should not be members, but it is not clear that they are prevented from being so. They should certainly not take part in any discussion from which they would receive a benefit. It may be more useful to have them 'in attendance' at the meeting, rather than members of the PCC.

A more common and more complex issue arises over organists. Organists are commonly engaged through an agreement whereby they are self-employed.[52] They are, therefore, not em-

---

47 Parochial Church Councils (Powers) Measure 1956, s4.
48 See Chapter 3.
49 Parsonages Measure 1938, s1.
50 Repair of Benefice Buildings Measure 1972, s5.
51 Parochial Church Councils (Powers) Measure 1956, s6.
52 The model contract is by The Incorporated Society of Musicians.

ployees of the PCC,[53] but they do have a financial benefit. Here it may be less inappropriate for them to be on the PCC, although they should still avoid being involved in any debate by which they would benefit.[54]

What happens when ...

... we can't find enough people?

The number of people to be elected to a PCC is a maximum. It is not, therefore, a legal crisis if there are not enough people to fill the places. However, it is always good to try to find people who are suitable to serve on the PCC as this encourages a sense of collaboration and shared ministry in the parish.

... the minister does not call a PCC meeting?

It is the duty of the minister to convene meetings of the PCC. If he or she fails to do so a formal request may be made by not less than one-third of the members of the PCC. If notice of a meeting is not given by the minister within seven days of such a request the members who made the request may lawfully convene a meeting, whether or not the minister agrees. They would need to make sure that proper notice of any such meeting is given.[55]

Resources you should have at your fingertips

Church Representation Rules[56]

---

53 A recent Employment Tribunal decision has suggested that such organists may be employees, despite having 'self-employment' contracts. The decision is not finalized at the time of writing.

54 For a discussion of this issue see *Legal Opinions concerning the Church of England*, p. 139.

55 Church Representation Rules, Appx II, para. 3.

56 See the longer note in Chapter 4 regarding latest versions.

Useful links

There are a number of books which give guidance on PCC matters including:

- Kenneth M. Macmorran and Timothy Briden, *Handbook for Churchwardens and Parochial Church Councillors*, London, Continuum, 2007.

- John Pitchford, *ABC for the PCC: A Handbook for Church Council Members*, London, Continuum, 2008..

- James Behrens, *Practical Church Management* (2nd edition), Leominster, Gracewing, 2005.

6

Baptisms

A possible scenario

A lady arrives at your doorstep on your day off. She has a toddler by her side and a baby in the pushchair. 'I want to get him done on Sunday', she announces, without formality or fear. What do you need to know?

What you need to know

All clergy, preferably with their PCC, need to work out a parish baptism policy and to a large degree this will be influenced by theology. However, it is important to know and understand the legal boundaries of the Church of England.

The canons state that baptism should usually be in public worship and in the main service of the day when the greatest number of people come together. This is so that the congregation may witness the baptism and be helped to remember their own profession of faith.[1] The canons then speak of the baptism of infants and of adults (quaintly described as 'those of riper years'). Clearly, when we look at the Bible, we find that the norm was for converts to be baptized as a sign of their adult profession of faith, but there are examples of whole families being baptized together and it is from this that we have developed the practice of infant baptism. There is an assumed duty on the minister to conduct a baptism when an adult requests to be baptized and a clear duty not to refuse to baptize an infant.[2]

---

1 Canon B21.
2 Canon B22(4).

What happens in practice?

The scenario at the head of this chapter is not unusual. The key to dealing with such enquiries both pastorally and lawfully is usually to arrange for a conversation with the person, when both are able to relax, and the minister can establish the necessary information. Avoid immediate reactions, such as 'That should be no problem' until you have enough information to know whether that is the case. A basic baptism enquiry form can be useful, as this will help a minister to remember to ask all the right questions at the initial stage and avoid frustration and disappointment at a later date.

Administration

It is always useful for a minister to set up a simple administrative system for dealing with baptism enquiries. A form should enable the minister to have all the right information in one place. It should include space for the full names of each parent (or guardian or person having custody) and the child, the date of birth, address, and the occupation of each of the parents. All this information will be needed for the register. It will also be useful to have a telephone number and an email address. There may also need to be space for details of any agreed dates, notes from any preparation visits or courses to be attended, full names and addresses of godparents, details of any brothers and sisters, any requests which may be made for particular hymns during the service and the approximate number of guests who may be attending. If this information is all on one form, which can easily be designed on a computer, then it will have all that is needed to guide each enquirer through the stages of initial enquiry, baptism visits, preparation, the service, and follow-up.

Preparation

Ministers must instruct adults who are to be baptized in the principles of the Christian religion, and encourage them to prepare themselves to receive the sacrament with repentance and faith.[3]

---

3 Canon B24(1).

By implication, they should also instruct parents and godparents as to the meaning of the baptism, although it is not stated as a direct injunction.[4]

At least a week before the baptism of an adult the minister must notify the bishop.[5] Every adult who is baptized must be confirmed by the bishop as soon after their baptism as conveniently possible so that they may be admitted to Holy Communion.[6]

Godparents and sponsors

So far as infant baptism is concerned, due notice must be given to the minister[7] and the minister must instruct the parents that the same responsibility rests on them as on the godparents.[8] The godparents (and presumably, therefore, also parents) must be people who will faithfully fulfil their responsibilities both by their care for the children committed to their charge and by the example of their own godly living.[9] No one may be a godparent who has not been baptized and confirmed. The minister has power to dispense with the requirement of confirmation, but not the requirement that they be baptized.[10]

For every child to be baptized there should be at least three godparents, two of the same sex as the child and one of the opposite sex. The minimum requirement is one godfather and one godmother. Parents may be godparents for their own children, provided that there is least one other godparent.[11]

For adults, godparents are not required. Instead, the adult should choose sponsors. These should be people who will present them at the font and afterwards remind them of their Christian profession and duties.[12]

---

4 Canon B22(4).
5 Canon B24(2).
6 Canon B24(3).
7 Canon B22(1).
8 Canon B22(3).
9 Canon B23(2).
10 Canon B23(4).
11 Canon B23(1).
12 Canon B23(3).

Fees and registration

It is unlawful for a minister to charge a fee for baptism.[13] A fee may be charged for a certificate of baptism and for a search of the baptism registers.[14] It would be unusual but not unlawful to charge this fee at the time of the baptism; it is usually only charged for producing a certificate at a later date. When a baptism has taken place it should be registered.[15] A register book must be provided by the parish.[16]

Follow-up

There is nothing in church law which talks about follow-up. However, in the same way that the church hopes that the family will take seriously the responsibility they have taken on in baptism, so too the church has a responsibility to be alongside the family in support and encouragement. In parishes where I have worked we have arranged for someone from the church to follow up infant baptisms with a visit to invite the parents to explore their faith further through Alpha Courses and with the Mother and Toddler Group. The Mothers' Union took on delivery of a birthday card to the family on the child's birthday for the first five years. Towards the end of that time another visit was arranged to invite the child to attend Sunday School. Mobility can be a problem here, but even if a proportion of people have moved by this time it is worth the effort of contacting those who have not.

For adults who are baptized it can be worth finding a way to encourage sponsors to take seriously their promise to remind the adult of the profession of faith. If church sponsors have been used they too should take every opportunity to follow up.

---

13 Baptismal Fees Abolition Act 1872, s1.

14 Ecclesiastical Fees Measure 1986 and the current Parochial Fees Order (usually revised annually by General Synod).

15 Parochial Records and Registers Measure 1978, s2(1) and Canon B39.

16 Canon F11.

FAQs

What are the minimum requirements for a baptism to be valid?

The absolute minimum requirement for Christian baptism to be valid is the use of water and for the baptism to be in the name of the Father, the Son and the Holy Spirit.[17] It is, however, unusual for this bare legal minimum to be applied or appropriate.

When can I defer a baptism?

A minister can only delay baptism for the purpose of preparing or instructing the parents or godparents. However, there must not be an undue delay, and if there is the parents may apply to the bishop, who will, after consultation with the minister, give such directions as he thinks fit.[18]

Can a reader baptize?

No. The only lay person who normally may be authorized to baptize is a deaconess, who may be authorized to do so in the absence of the minister.[19] A lay person may, however, perform a baptism in an emergency.[20] This usually means imminent danger to the child, not that the minister went on holiday and forgot to organize someone to do the baptism!

Is it lawful to baptize an adult by immersion?

Yes, there is no reason why not. The history of the Church of England assumes infant baptism as a norm, but in today's society it is increasingly the case that older children or adults are baptized, and in these circumstances full immersion is a powerful

---

17 Rubric in the Book of Common Prayer at the end of the service of Private Baptism of Infants.

18 Canons B22(4) and B22(2).

19 Canon D1(4)(b).

20 *Common Worship Initiation Services* rubric to the service for emergency baptism.

visual depiction of dying and rising with Christ. *Common Worship: Initiation Services* includes provision for 'clothing' after a baptism on the assumption that baptism by immersion is used in some places.

When can a baptized child receive Holy Communion?

Generally the assumption in the Church of England is that people should be confirmed before they receive communion.[21] The Book of Common Prayer does allow for people to receive if they are 'ready and desirous of confirmation'. However, in 1996 the House of Bishops prepared *Guidelines for the Admission of Baptized Persons to Holy Communion before Confirmation*. These guidelines allow parishes, with the consent of both the minister and the PCC, to apply to the bishop for permission to introduce the practice of allowing communion before confirmation. Some dioceses made small amendments to the national guidelines, so you need to check with your diocesan office. There is always a careful preparation procedure to follow. The latest version of the national regulations (2006) is available on the Church of England web-site.

At what age can children answer for themselves?

As a child grows up it may not be appropriate for the parents and godparents to answer on their behalf without them also being involved. This situation is increasingly common. The services include provision for children to answer for themselves, together with the parents and godparents, but when is it right for this to happen? There is not a legal answer to this question. It is a matter of discernment in each situation, and every child will be different. The question they are asked in the service is: *Is this your faith?* The response is: *This is my faith.* If a minister believes the child is able to answer this with an integrity appropriate to their age then it is in order to ask them the question at the service.

---

21 Canon B15A.

Can a child be baptized against a parent's wishes?

No. Where a child is old enough to answer for themselves they make the declarations with the parents and godparents. Liturgically, this assumes that the parents are also taking part. Legally, it would not be appropriate to proceed with the baptism of a child against the wishes of a parent.

What happens when ...

... the family does not live in our parish?

A minister who intends to baptize any infant whose parents are residing outside the parish, unless at least one parent has their name on the church electoral roll, must not proceed without having sought the goodwill of the minister of the parish in which the parents reside.[22] This does not seem to insist that the baptism can only go ahead with the goodwill of the other parish priest, but generally it would be good professional practice to respect the response that is given by the other parish priest.

... they want to be baptized elsewhere?

The minister of the parish in which a family lives has the right to be consulted and asked for his or her goodwill. As in the above answer, the issue here is about how parishes work together in a locality and respect one another's different policies. My own view is that I always give permission for people to be baptized elsewhere, as I am pleased that they want baptism at all. I have done this even when a neighbouring parish will habitually not give goodwill for baptisms to take place when the shoe is on the other foot.

... there are no qualifying godparents?

On the face of it the parents need to provide godparents; but what if they have no one, or at least no one who fits the criteria? This

---

22 Canon B22(5).

may be a pastoral opportunity for the parish. Perhaps the parish could offer to provide some godparents who will be able to stay in touch with the family and support them in bringing the child up in the faith.

... a godparent cannot be present?

There is a long-standing precedent of families being allowed to present a 'proxy' godparent when their intended godparent cannot be present. This is not really a good practice, as the baptism service assumes an interaction between the minister and the godparents in which they agree to fulfil their responsibilities. There is a fascinating discussion in one of the legal text books as to whether it would be acceptable for parents to be present by video link.[23] Generally, while it has long been done, using a proxy godparent is better avoided.

Resources you should have at your fingertips

- *Common Worship: Initiation Services.*
- Canons B21–B25.
- Canon F11.
- Parish baptism policy and forms.

Useful links

- *Common Worship* liturgy may be downloaded from www.cofe.anglican.org/worship/liturgy/commonworship/texts/index.html
- The House of Bishops' *Guidelines on the Admission of Baptized Persons to Holy Communion before Confirmation* is available at www.cofe.anglican.org/info/education/children/childrencommunion.doc

---

23 *Legal Opinions Concerning the Church of England*, pp. 338–41.

7

Marriage

A possible scenario

It's 5.45 pm on Sunday afternoon and you are about to leave for Evensong. The phone rings. It's a member of your congregation. 'Good news,' she says, 'my youngest, Darren, came round for lunch and he and Michelle (from Spain) told me they plan to get married next spring. I thought it would speed things up if I had a word with you and booked the church myself.' How do you respond?

What you need to know

What is marriage?

Marriage in the Church of England is governed by canon and by the Marriage Act 1949. It is helpful to start by knowing and understanding how the church defines marriage, not least given that our society is confused on the matter. The Church of England's official description of marriage is that it is a permanent and lifelong union, of one man with one woman, to the exclusion of all others on either side.[1]

When can a marriage take place?

The law does not allow marriage to take place at any time of the day. A marriage service may only take place between the hours of

---

1 Canon B30(1).

eight in the morning and six in the afternoon.[2] It can take place on any day of the week, including Sunday, although whether a minister will agree to do so will depend upon other commitments.

Who may marry?

When an application for marriage is made, the minister has a duty to ask enough questions to ensure that there is no legal impediment either to the marriage or to performing the wedding.[3] The main reasons a marriage may not be possible include the following: no one who is under 16 years of age may marry;[4] a minister may not marry two people either of whom is under 18 years of age except with the consent of the parents of a person under 18;[5] no one may marry within the relationships expressed in the following table.[6]

A table of kindred and affinity

A man may not marry his	A woman may not marry her
mother	father
adoptive mother	adoptive father
former adoptive mother	former adoptive father
daughter	son
adoptive daughter	adoptive son
former adoptive daughter	former adoptive son
father's mother	father's father
mother's mother	mother's father
son's daughter	son's son
daughter's daughter	daughter's son

---

2 Canon B35(3).

3 Canon B33.

4 Canon B31(1).

5 Canon B32.

6 Canon B31(2) and Marriage (Prohibited Degrees of Relationship) Act 1986 as amended by the Children Act 1975.

sister	brother
wife's mother	husband's father
wife's daughter	husband's son
father's wife	mother's husband
son's wife	daughter's husband
father's father's wife	father's mother's husband
mother's father's wife	mother's mother's husband
wife's father's mother	husband's mother's father
wife's mother's mother	husband's father's father
wife's daughter's daughter	husband's daughter's son
wife's son's daughter	husband's son's son
wife's son's daughter	husband's daughter's son
son's son's wife	daughter's daughter's husband
father's sister	father's brother
mother's sister	mother's brother
brother's daughter	brother's son
sister's daughter	sister's son
daughter of a former wife	son of a former husband
former wife of father	former husband of mother
former wife of father's father	former husband of father's mother
former wife of mother's father	former husband of mother's mother
daughter of son of former wife	son of son of former husband
daughter of daughter of former wife	son of daughter of former husband
mother of former wife	father of former husband
former wife of son	former daughter of husband

In this table the term 'brother' includes a brother of the half-blood, and the term 'sister' includes a sister of the half-blood. It is worth noting that this table is more fulsome than that in Canon

B31 and includes additions made by subsequent legislation. The table should be displayed in every church.[7]

Preliminaries

A marriage according to the rites of the Church of England may only be solemnized (that is to say conducted) after one of the four possible 'preliminaries' has taken place. These are four methods by which a check can be conducted to ensure that the marriage is lawful. They are the calling of banns, a special licence of marriage granted by the Archbishop of Canterbury,[8] a licence granted by the bishop (called a 'common licence'), or a certificate issued by a superintendent registrar.[9] When a couple first approaches a minister to enquire about marriage, one of the first steps is to decide which of these processes for the preliminaries will be used. It is probably most usual for the marriage to be conducted after banns, and that is a good starting assumption. Then, in the light of the advice which follows, a minister will need to be alert to any issue which may mean banns cannot be called. In that case the minister can consider which alternative method is appropriate. It is important for ministers to be aware of the potential issues right from the start, as it can cause problems if he or she only realizes at a later stage that there is need to use a different method of preliminary. Full details of rules and regulations regarding marriage under these four headings can be found in *Anglican Marriage in England and Wales: A Guide to the Law for Clergy* (see below). However, a brief overview of the legal issues follows.

Marriage after banns

This is the most common method by which a marriage is conducted. Banns need to be called in each place where the couple have a relevant connection: that is, in the parish or both parishes in which the parties reside, and in the parish where either of

---

7 Canon B31(2).
8 Ecclesiastical Licences Act 1533.
9 Canon B34(1).

them is a member of the electoral roll (if the marriage is to take place there).[10] The minister of the parish in which the marriage is to take place will usually take responsibility for seeing that the banns are called there. The couple must take responsibility for arranging banns to be called elsewhere, if advised by the minister. It may be helpful for the minister to have a system which can check that it is happening three to four months before the wedding. After all, the couple are new at this!

The minister is entitled to receive notice in writing seven days before the first publication of banns, which must give the full names of the persons to be married, their addresses, and the length of time that they have lived there.[11] This is a formal requirement, but it is much more common for the minister who is to conduct the wedding to have more than enough notice, often a couple of years. The notice is likely to be shorter in any parish where banns need to be called but the marriage is to take place elsewhere (I always refer to these as 'away banns'). However, even if short notice is given, most ministers will do all they can to help a couple along the way, as they are usually in unfamiliar territory, and it should be second nature to the minister.

Banns are to be published on three Sundays preceding the marriage, usually during the main morning service. If there is no morning service on a Sunday on which the banns are to be published, it is permissible for them to be called in the evening service.[12]

Every parish must keep a register of banns, into which the details are written and from which they are read.[13] Usually the banns must be read (that is, called or published) by the minister.[14] Banns of marriage may be published by a lay person when no member of the clergy is present.[15] Where this happens, the lay person signs the banns register as the officiating minister, but the duty of entering the banns and of issuing certificates of publication

---

10 Marriage Act 1949, s14.
11 Marriage Act 1949, s8.
12 Marriage Act 1949, s7(1).
13 Marriage Act 1949, s7(3).
14 Marriage Act 1949, s9(1).
15 Marriage Act 1949, s9(2).

(which should always be signed by a minister) remains with the incumbent.[16]

Marriage after common licence

If a common licence is required the minister will need to advise the couple that this is so and help them to go through the process. Application for a common licence must be made to a surrogate, an officer of the chancellor appointed for this purpose. It is usually one of the clergy of the deanery. Details of local surrogates are listed in diocesan year books. The surrogate does the paperwork, and passes the papers on to the diocesan registry who will then issue the licence.

A common licence can only be granted if one of the parties has resided for at least the fifteen days in the parish in which the marriage is to take place before the licence is issued or is on the church electoral roll of that parish.[17] The granting of a common licence is discretionary and not a matter of right. A common licence will not normally be granted where neither of the parties has been baptized. The process includes swearing an affidavit. This is a legal document which sets out certain information about the couple. They then take an oath that the contents of the document are true. It is often used when there is some reason why that element will be useful, for example where one party is a foreign national who wishes to be sure that their marriage will be lawful in their home country (see below).

Marriage after special licence

Once again it will be the minister's responsibility to help the couple through this process. For a marriage by special licence, application should be made to the Faculty Office.[18] When an initial enquiry is made the appropriate forms are sent out by the Faculty Office, together with helpful guidelines, so it may be

---

16 Marriage Act 1949, s11(4).

17 Marriage Act 1949, s16.

18 1 The Sanctuary, Westminster, London SW1P 3JT. Tel: 020 7222 5381.

worth getting hold of the papers in good time, if this looks like a possible method to be used in a particular case. A special licence is issued only in unusual circumstances, and it enables the parties to be married at any time or place in England without previous residence in the district.[19] One party must be baptized for a special licence to be granted.

Marriage after superintendent registrar's certificate

In certain circumstances,[20] it may be possible for marriage to be solemnized on the authority of a (secular) superintendent registrar's certificate.[21] It is rarely used for Church of England marriages.

Residence

For all these preliminaries (except a special licence) there is a residence requirement. Parishioners (including those on the church electoral roll) have the right to marry in the church of the parish in which they are resident, but they do not have the right to be married in any other parish church. This is not easily understood by people who can buy almost anything for the wedding except the right to have it in any church they choose.

It is not possible to define exhaustively what is meant by residence. It is a question of fact, to be decided in the circumstances of each case, whether or not a person lives within a parish. It can be said, however, that renting a room and leaving luggage there without occupation is not a residential qualification within the meaning of the Marriage Act. To avoid getting embroiled or duped I usually simply ask the question right from the first contact in the form 'Where do you actually live?' It is a simple enough question and usually gets to the facts or reveals any ambiguity. It is the duty of the clergy to inquire whether there is a legal impediment to the marriage, but unless they have good reason to do so,

---

19 Marriage Act 1949, s79 and Ecclesiastical Licences Act 1533.
20 See *Anglican Marriage in England and Wales: A Guide to the Law for Clergy*, section 8. See below, p. 69.
21 Marriage Act 1949, s26.

they are not under an obligation to check the truth of what they are told about residence. Ultimately the couple are responsible for the statements they make.

Changes in the law regarding residence

The Church of England has recently addressed the issue of rights to marriage afresh. As from 1 October 2008 the right to marry has been extended. The new regulations are designed to make it easier for couples to get married in a church that has a special meaning for them. Provided the church is available, couples will have a right to get married in:

- the parish where they reside;
- the parish where they were baptized and/or confirmed;
- a parish in which they have lived for six months or more, at any time during their lives;
- a parish in which they have attended worship for at least six months at any time;
- the parish in which their parents lived or worshipped (during the child's lifetime);
- the parish in which their parents or grandparents were married.[22]

Marriages where one of the above special connections is claimed will normally take place by banns. Banns would need to be called in the parish in which either party resides and in the parish in which the marriage is to take place. Suitable forms are on the Church of England web-site.

Administration

It is useful for a minister or parish administrator to set up a system and have some forms available to ensure that the parish has

---

22 See Church of England Marriage Measure 2008, and guidance material which can be found at www.cofe.anglican.org/info/socialpublic/marriagefamily/marriageanddivorce/marriagemeasure.

all the right information and that each couple is dealt with in the same way. There is a form that can be purchased which mirrors the information in the marriage register and this may be useful. I personally find a much more fulsome form is more helpful, covering all the statutory information which will be required for the registers, but also covering all the administrative steps, such as wedding interview, service planning, marriage preparation, rehearsal and follow-up. All this can easily be created on a computer on two sides of A4 paper, and then the paperwork does all the hard work.

Services

When a minister solemnizes a marriage one of the lawful services must be used.[23] This means the service in the Book of Common Prayer, the *Series One Solemnization of Matrimony,* or service in the *Common Worship: Pastoral Services* book.[24] Note that the 1928 Prayer Book service has never been an authorized service. There is authority in the canons to make minor variations to the service, but care must be taken that such changes are minor and consistent with the doctrine of the Church of England.[25]

The decision as to which form of service is to be used is made by the minister who is to conduct the service, but if any of the people concerned object beforehand to the use of the service selected by the minister, and the person and the minister cannot agree, the matter must be referred to the bishop of the diocese for his decision.[26] It is for the minister of the parish to decide what music may be played, what hymns or anthems may be sung, or what furnishings or flowers may be placed in the church for the occasion.[27] Clearly a minister will want to take everyone's wishes into account but the law is clear as to who has the final say.

---

23 Canon B1(2).
24 Authorized under Canon B2.
25 Canon B5(1) and B5(3).
26 Canon B3(4).
27 Canon B35(5).

Marriage registration

After a marriage has taken place it must be registered by the person who officiated at the ceremony.[28] There is a guide to registration which should be followed closely and carefully (see below). Each quarter the incumbent must make a return to the superintendent registrar containing a certified copy of every new entry in the marriage registers.[29] Failure to do so is a fineable offence.[30]

Fees

The legal fees for a marriage cover the publication of the banns, the marriage service and a certificate of marriage. There is also a fee for calling banns and issuing a banns certificate when the wedding is to be elsewhere. These fees are fixed centrally and a fee sheet is sent annually to all clergy with their pay slip. This can cause difficulties for self-supporting ministers, but it is available for download from the Church of England web-site. A parish may charge further fees for any extras for the service, such as a choir, organist, bell-ringers, special lighting, fees for video recording and so on. It is important that this is clearly communicated to those booking weddings. These extras should usually be approved by the PCC (rather than the incumbent alone) as they will be the recipients of these fees.

Some of the fee is due to the PCC and some is due to the incumbent, so a minister needs to have a system in place to deal with the fees accurately and promptly. Fees form part of a minister's income.[31]

FAQs

What must a minister say when calling banns?

It is important when calling banns to do so in the correct form. After all, this is the legal preliminary to the marriage and it

---

28 Marriage Act 1949, s53.
29 Marriage Act 1949, s57.
30 Marriage Act 1949, s76.
31 See Chapter 16.

must be right. The only valid wording of banns is either those in the Book of Common Prayer or in *Common Worship: Pastoral Services*. The latter is more often used. The form of words is:

> I publish the banns of marriage between NN of ... and NN of ...
> This is the *first / second / third* time of asking.
> If any of you know any reason in law why they may not marry each other you are to declare it.
> We pray for these couples (*or N and N*) as they prepare for their wedding(s).

It is not necessary to say whether people are single, widowed or previously married when you read banns, even though it is recorded in the banns book.

What happens when a parish does not have a service every week?

Banns must be called on three Sundays in the relevant parish, but not necessarily on three successive Sundays. If, for example a small church in a rural benefice has a service every fortnight it would be acceptable for the banns to be called at three services in that church, even if that was over slightly longer a period than is normal.

For how long are banns valid?

Banns are valid for three months from the date of publication, which usually means from the third date on which they are called.[32] Common licences are also valid for three months from the date of issue.[33] A special licence will contain the date to which it is valid. The officiating minister may receive a banns certificate from another parish,[34] or a licence from elsewhere, and it is the minister's duty to check that the marriage is within the prescribed period for which the certificate or licence is valid.

---

32 Marriage Act 1949, s12.
33 Marriage Act 1949, s16.
34 Marriage Act 1949, s11.

What about 'gay marriage'?

It is worth pointing out that a civil partnership between two persons of the same sex (permitted by law in this country)[35] is not a marriage. It is common usage for it to be referred to as gay marriage, but this is clearly theological nonsense.[36] That does not mean that such partnerships may not be valid in their own right, but they are not marriage.

Can a minister do a civil partnership?

No. There is no lawful Church of England service for such a thing, and the civil registration service cannot be taken by a minister. The registration of a civil partnership may not include any religious service.[37]

Can a minister take a wedding anywhere?

No. A marriage conducted according to the rites and ceremonies of the Church of England should usually be in a church.[38] There are a few exceptions to this, for which see 'the Purple Book' (see page 69).

Can anyone take a wedding in our church?

Generally the marriage must be solemnized and registered by a clerk in holy orders of the Church of England. The couple may come to a minister and ask if a relative or friend who is a minister may take the wedding. It is important to establish their proper credentials before answering the question. They should only take the wedding if they are a Church of England minister and even

---

35 Civil Partnerships Act 2004.

36 Although some consider it is not a legal nonsense. See J. Humphreys, 'The Civil Partnership Act, Same Sex Marriage and the Church of England', *Ecclesiastical Law Journal*, 8 (2006), p. 289.

37 Civil Partnerships Act 2004, s2(5).

38 Marriage Act 1949, s12.

then the minister of the parish will want to ensure that things such as registration, for which they will be answerable later, are done properly. Other people may be permitted to assist in the marriage but not to solemnize it. As a minimum, the officiating minister should read the opening charge to the couple, receive the vows, pronounce the couple man and wife and pronounce the nuptial blessing.[39]

Can a deacon take a marriage?

Yes. There are guidelines issued by the archbishops, available in the supplementary material at the rear of the canons: www.cofe. anglican.org/about/churchlawlegis/canons.

What if one (or both) of the parties is a foreign national?

Where either of the parties is a foreign national, it is strongly recommended that Church of England marriage should be by common licence, especially if either party is a national of a country outside the Old Commonwealth, the European Union or the United States, for their own protection.

Home Office Regulations issued in 2005[40] have restricted access to marriage in register offices for those who are not British citizens. This restriction has resulted in a dramatic fall in the number of register office marriages taking place between non-British citizens. However, the restriction does not apply to Church of England marriages. Consequently there has been a related increase in the number of such couples who are now approaching clergy to be married in Church of England churches, especially in multi-cultural urban areas. In such cases advice should be sought from your diocesan registry. It may well be that there is no reason why the marriage may not proceed, but care is needed in such cases.

---

39 See the Purple Book.
40 The Immigration (Procedure for Marriage) Regulations 2005.

Can a minister take a blessing service after a civil marriage?

Yes.[41] There is a service commended for use in *Common Worship: Pastoral Services*. This may be after a ceremony at a register office or at approved premises and should usually take place in a church. (The Marriage Act now allows for civil weddings to take place on 'approved premises', such as hotels and country houses.)[42]

The Act provides that no religious service shall be used at a marriage at approved premises.[43] Requests are sometimes made for clergy to attend and say prayers after the marriage service. This is a sensitive matter. Some bishops advise clergy not to offer prayer or a blessing at the hotel or approved premises if requested to do so. In such a context it would be too easy for the proper seriousness of the spiritual dimension of Christian marriage to be downgraded. The bishops do recognize that there may well be pastoral opportunities in such a request which may be used, and it would be wise to seek the advice of your bishop on this.

Must a minister do wedding preparation?

It is the minister's duty, when application is made for a marriage, to explain the Church's doctrine of marriage, and the need of God's grace in marriage.[44] This is clearly an opportunity for marriage preparation and should be taken up fully.

Does one party need to be baptized?

No, not if the marriage is to take place after banns. The answer may be yes if the marriage is to be by licence, so beware!

---

41 Canon B36.
42 Marriage Act 1949, s46A.
43 Marriage Act 1949, s46B(4).
44 Canon B30(3).

What happens when ...

... *one party lives abroad?*

If either of the parties to a marriage in England has a foreign domicile (that is, they are British citizens but their fixed and permanent home is abroad), they should ensure that the legal requirements of their country of residence are observed. This will ensure there is no risk about the recognition of a Church of England marriage in their country of residence. In such cases it is wise always to consult your diocesan registry. It may also be wise to get the couple to consult the embassy. There is often no problem about a Church of England marriage being recognized in a foreign country, but better to be careful than sorry.

... *one party has been previously married?*

The clergy of the Church of England cannot be compelled to solemnize the marriage of a divorced person whose former spouse is still living, or to permit the marriage to be solemnized in the church of which s/he is the minister.[45]

The Church's current discipline on the remarriage of divorced persons is set out in the House of Bishops' Advice issued in 2003 (see below). This guidance sets out a number of issues and questions clergy may wish to address with couples intending to be married in these circumstances. There is an application form that is recommended for use in all cases. It may be helpful to have a PCC discussion, so that you know that your PCC understands the issues, but note that the final decision on remarriage of divorcees must in every case be a matter for the individual clergy concerned. Clergy may wish to refer cases to the bishop for advice, but they are likely simply to be told that the bishop will support them as they make their decision. It is vital, under human rights legislation, that only the minister responsible makes the final decision. It is also essential that whatever approach clergy adopt on the issue generally, they apply their own policy consistently. In case of doubt, consult the diocesan registrar.

---

45 Matrimonial Causes Act 1965, s8.

... *someone objects to the calling of banns?*

The only valid objection to the calling of banns itself is on the grounds that the person is a minor and does not have the consent of their parents to the calling of banns. Any other objection would not invalidate the banns, although it may affect the wedding. The form of the banns is to ask that anyone who knows a reason in law why the couple may not marry should say so. The objection, if raised, is more likely to be an objection to the wedding than an objection to the banns being called. The grounds on which someone can object are the same as for an objection at the wedding itself (see next question). Any such objection should be noted in public, and then investigated in private.

... *someone objects at the wedding?*

There are very few valid grounds for such objections, despite the fun which the film industry has had with this idea. The objection must allege that there is legal impediment to the marriage, which may mean that the parties are not respectively male and female, one party is under age, or is within the prohibited degrees, or is already married. No other objection clearly meets the grounds that there is a legal impediment.

In the unlikely event of an objection, the minister should retire to the vestry with the person who objects. They should be asked to explain their objection and the minister will have to decide if it is a lawful objection. According to the rubric in the Book of Common Prayer, if the minister decides there is a prima facie case they may ask the person to give a cash surety against any loss suffered by the parties and then the ceremony should be deferred. If the minister decides there is no case, then the wedding proceeds, and so long as the minister has listened carefully and made an honest decision there should be no further comeback against him or her, even if it was later discovered that the objection was valid. Don't stay awake at night worrying about the possibility. It has not happened to many people!

... someone forgets to get banns called?

This will depend on how much time is available. It is usually possible to get a common licence at fairly short notice where the necessary residence and baptism qualifications apply. A special licence may also be obtainable at short notice (on condition that one party is baptized) so long as someone is prepared to go to London to get it. The best thing to do is ring the registry clerk as soon as the problem emerges. While responsibility for arranging away banns rests with the couple, it is wise for the minister's administrative system to have a check point a few weeks before the wedding which will bring the problem to light early enough for it to be dealt with.

... an error is made in the marriage registers?

There is detailed advice about this in 'the Green Book'. If the error is spotted before the registration is completed it is relatively simple, following some clear rules, to correct it. If it is not spotted until later this can be more difficult. It may be necessary to get the officiating minister, the couple and all the witnesses together in order to sort it out, so care is always worthwhile. Consult the superintendent registrar if you are unsure what to do.

Resources you should have at your fingertips

* All clergy should have a copy of two key guides on this subject. The first is called *Anglican Marriage in England and Wales: A Guide to the Law for Clergy*. This is available from the Faculty Office, 1 The Sanctuary, Westminster, London SW1P 3JT. Tel: 020 7222 5381. It is sometimes referred to as 'the Purple Book'. The second is *Suggestions for the Guidance of the Clergy with regard to the Marriage and Registration Acts*. This may well be available from your local registrar of births deaths and marriages. If not, it is available from the Registrar-General, Smedley Hydro, Trafalgar Road, Southport PR8 2HH. Tel: 0151 471 4803. It is sometimes known as 'the Green Book'.

- The House of Bishops' Advice to Clergy concerning marriage and divorce: available in the supplementary material at the rear of the Canons, www.cofe.anglican.org/about/churchlawlegis/canons

- Marriage Act 1949.

- Canons B30–B36.

- Canon F11.

- Your parish administration system.

Useful links

- The marriage service and other linked material is in *Common Worship: Pastoral Services*, which can be downloaded from www.cofe.anglican.org/worship/liturgy/commonworship/texts/index.html

- Marriage preparation and marriage support web-sites include: www.marriageresource.org.uk/
www.marriage-preparation.co.uk/
themarriagecourse.org/

- The Church of England Weddings web page has general information about weddings in church: www.cofe.anglican.org/lifeevents/weddings

- The Faculty Office in Westminster has a web-site at: http://www.facultyoffice.org.uk/

- The General Register Office web-site also has lots of useful information: www.gro.gov.uk

- A copy of each year's legal fee sheet is available from www.cofe.anglican.org/lifeevents/ministry/workofmindiv/dracsc

8

Funerals and Churchyards

A possible scenario

Mrs Jones' father had been ill for some time, so he moved out from London so that she could look after him in her home. After a brief time he has died and Mrs Jones contacts you to ask about having a service at the crematorium, his ashes buried in the churchyard, and a small stone in the shape of a book placed over the ashes. What do you need to be aware of?

What you need to know

On death and dying

The Church of England's understanding of ministry at the time of death has recently been much enhanced by the range of material available in *Common Worship: Pastoral Services*. This book contains a range of services providing for ministry at the time of death, receiving the coffin into the church, the funeral service, ministry at home after a service and memorial services. As can be seen, the thinking behind this is that there is much more to bereavement ministry than a funeral service alone. There is provision for ministry before and after the funeral service and these services should be used as widely and wisely as possible. However, much of what follows relates specifically to funerals and churchyards.

Who may be buried

Every parishioner and inhabitant in a parish, as well as anyone dying within a parish, has the right to be buried in the parish churchyard or burial ground if it is open.[1] This extends to the right to burial of cremated remains.[2] A person who has their name on the electoral roll of a parish at the date of death has the same rights as a parishioner.[3] The minister of a parish may also take a funeral service at a cemetery or crematorium situated in another parish for the same group of people (that is parishioners, those who die in the parish or those on the electoral roll).[4]

Who may take a service

The Church of England burial service should normally be led by an ordained person, but the bishop, with the consent of the minister of the parish, may authorize a deaconess,[5] a reader[6] or a lay worker[7] to lead the service. Even when they are authorized by the bishop, the family have the right to object to a lay person taking a funeral. In most cases they are rarely asked, but if an objection is raised it should be respected. There is also provision for other people to conduct a burial in a churchyard, with or without a religious service, if those responsible for the burial so request.[8] This is to protect the parishioner's right to burial in the churchyard if they are not members of the Church of England. Thus it would be lawful, for example, for the local Methodist minister to take a service in his or her church and then to bury in the Church of England churchyard or for a humanist minister to take a service at the graveside.

Cremation

Until about a century ago burial was the norm following death, but in recent years cremation has been much more common and

---

1 Canon B38.

2 Church of England (Miscellaneous Provisions) Measure 1992, s3.

3 Canon B38(2).

4 Church of England (Miscellaneous Provisions) Measure 1992, s2(2).

5 Canon D1(4).

6 Canon E4(2A).

7 Canon E7(5)(c).

8 Burial Laws Amendment Act 1880.

in some areas is the only option available. Cremation is lawful in connection with Christian burial.[9] When a body is to be cremated, the funeral service may precede, accompany, or follow the cremation and may be held either in the church or at the crematorium. The ashes of a cremated body should be reverently disposed of by a minister in a churchyard or other burial ground, in an area of land designated by the bishop for the purpose, or at sea.[10]

Services

When a minister buries in consecrated ground, one of the lawful services must be used.[11] There is authority in the canons to make minor variations to the service, but care must be taken that such changes are minor and not contrary to, or indicative of any departure from, the doctrine of the Church of England in any essential matter.[12] As well as the service in the Book of Common Prayer, the *Common Worship: Pastoral Services* book contains some services that are authorized and others that are commended for use.[13] The commended services may be used if the minister having cure of souls so decides.[14] The *Series One Burial Service* is also still authorized. If the burial is to take place in unconsecrated ground and the rites of the Church of England are to be used, the minister must first bless the grave.[15]

---

9 Canon B38(3).

10 Canon B38(4).

11 Canon B1(2).

12 Canons B5(1) and B5(3).

13 Authorized under Canon B2: The Outline Order for Funerals, The Funeral Service, The Funeral Service within a celebration of Holy Communion, The Blessing of a Grave, and The Burial of Ashes. Commended under Canon B2: Ministry at the Time of Death, Receiving the Coffin at Church before the Funeral, The Outline Order for the Funeral of a Child, The Outline Order for the Funeral of a Child within a celebration of Holy Communion, At Home After a Funeral, An Outline Order for a Memorial Service, An Outline Order for Memorial Service within a Celebration of Holy Communion, and Memorial Service: A Sample Service.

14 Canon B5(2).

15 Canon B38(5).

The choice as to which authorized form of service is to be used belongs to the officiating minister, though any people who are particularly involved are entitled to express their preferences beforehand and, whenever possible and appropriate, such preferences ought to be met. Opportunity should always be given for discussion beforehand between the minister and people who are particularly involved. If no agreement is reached, the matter must be referred to the bishop, whose decision is final.[16]

Authority to bury

Before a burial takes place, authority for the burial should be produced, usually by the undertaker. This will normally consist of a certificate from the registrar of deaths, or the coroner's burial order. It is always best practice also to ensure that the plate on the coffin or ashes casket matches the name of the deceased. Within 96 hours of a burial, the registrar of deaths must be notified of the details of the date and place of the burial. The detachable portion of the registrar's certificate (sometimes known as the 'green form') or the coroner's order may be used for this purpose. When ashes are to be buried the minister should be provided with a certificate of cremation. There is no 'return' required in this case.

Registration

When a burial or a burial of ashes has taken place it should be registered.[17] A register of burials should be provided by the parish and this should be used to register the service.[18] The parish should also have a register of burials of ashes and a register of faculties for reserved grave spaces (if any) together with a plan showing where the reserved spaces are located. There should also be a plan of the churchyard and this should be kept up to date.

---

16 Canon B3.
17 Parochial Records and Registers Measure 1978, s3.1 and Canon B39.
18 Canon F11.

Administration

It is again useful for a minister to set up a simple administrative system for dealing with funerals. A form should ensure that the minister has all the right information in one place. It should include space for the full names of the person who has died, their age, date of birth and date of death, any name they were usually known by, details of the next of kin and their contact information. It may be useful to include on the same form space for information regarding the funeral service, disposal of ashes or place of committal, and other relevant information ready for pastoral follow-up in the parish. If this information is all on one form, which can be easily designed on a computer, then this will guide a minister through the stages from initial contact through the service to follow-up.

Memorials

Although there are legal rights to burial and interment in a churchyard, they do not confer any right of ownership of the soil in which the burial and interment take place. This means that there is no right for anyone to place any item at or on a grave without permission. The person with the legal responsibility for making rules about memorials in churchyards is the chancellor of the diocese. The chancellor is entitled to allow the erection or removal of a memorial, kerb, ornament or inscription in a churchyard and such permission must be sought through an application for a faculty.[19]

However, chancellors usually delegate some of their authority to the incumbent or priest in charge of the parish (or in a vacancy to the rural dean). An incumbent or priest in charge may grant permission, after application on the approved form, for a memorial to be erected in a churchyard so long as the application is within the terms of the delegated authority from the chancellor.

If the application is outside the regulations then the form should be returned to the stonemasons advising them that a faculty must be applied for. Any person found responsible for the unlawful

---

19 For more information on faculties generally see Chapter 14.

introduction of a memorial of any kind into a churchyard may be ordered by the chancellor to pay the costs of removal and of legal proceedings compelling him to do so.[20] In any case of doubt the matter should be referred to the chancellor.

It is usual for the regulations to state that no memorial shall be introduced into a churchyard before six months have passed after the burial. This is to allow the ground to settle and avoid the costs of resetting the stone at a later date. It is worth noting that most chancellor's delegated authority does not extend to the removal of memorials. This always requires a faculty. Temporary removal (for example for cleaning, or for the addition of a further inscription approved under delegated authority) may be approved by the incumbent, but not permanent removal.

Burial of ashes

The right to burial of ashes is referred to above. Burial of ashes may also take place in a grave-space in a closed churchyard, but only with faculty permission. The cremated remains of a person may be buried in a grave-space already containing one or more bodies of relatives of that person. It is the responsibility of the person requesting an additional burial to ensure that the proposed burial is acceptable to all close members of the family or families concerned. Otherwise cremated remains will usually be buried in an area set aside by faculty for this purpose. The PCC may apply for a faculty to set aside such an area, and the faculty will state whether memorials of any sort are permissible within or on it. A faculty will also be required to establish a book of remembrance recording the names of those so interred. such a book would be in addition to the required register of burials of ashes.

Grave-space reservations

Grave-spaces may only be reserved by faculty. In practice, chancellors will generally only grant a faculty to reserve the space for

---

20 See *Re Icklesham Churchyard*, October 2007, Chichester Consistory Court.

a fixed period of years. In such cases it is within the chancellor's power to order that the applicant pay a sum of money to the PCC of the parish concerned as a contribution towards the cost of maintaining the churchyard.[21]

Fees

The fees chargeable for funeral and burial services and for the introduction of memorials into a churchyard are set centrally and no further fees should be charged. A fee sheet is sent annually to clergy. Part of the fees are due to the PCC and part to the incumbent.[22]

FAQs

Does a minister have to agree to include what the family wants in the service?

As set out above, the actual content of the service is at the discretion of the minister.[23] However, it is very common for the family to ask for particular words or music, and this should be given due consideration. It is the minister's duty to ensure that the service is reverent and seemly and is neither contrary to, nor indicative of any departure from, the doctrine of the Church of England in any essential matter.[24] The minister also has a duty to ensure that worship is appropriate to a solemn act of worship in the House of God.[25] This is sometimes not an easy tightrope to walk and requires pastoral sensitivity.

Is the minister in charge or is the undertaker?

The answer to this depends on circumstances. Good undertakers will make contact with a minister before making any firm

---

21 *Legal Opinions concerning the Church of England*, p. 214.
22 See Chapter 16, dealing with the fees.
23 Canon B3(4), and see Chapter 15.
24 Canon B5(3).
25 Canon B20(3).

arrangements, but this does not always happen for a range of reasons. Undertakers would no doubt also want me to add that responsible clergy should reply to answerphone messages promptly. The frustration can work in both directions. A good working relationship should be established with local undertakers. So far as the service itself is concerned, the minister is responsible for what happens in the church, but the undertakers also have responsibilities to their client. I have always followed the practice of walking beside the undertaker as far as the church or crematorium door, and then walking alone and in front once we are inside. This sends the quiet message that we are working together on the whole, but once inside I am in charge.

Where can a minister take a funeral service?

A minister is authorized to take a service according to the rites of the Church of England in a church, a churchyard, or at a cemetery or crematorium. Occasionally you may get a request to take a service in someone's back garden or elsewhere. A minister may not take a Church of England service in such places.[26]

Who is responsible for the maintenance of a churchyard?

The maintenance of an open or a closed churchyard is the responsibility of the PCC. If the churchyard is closed by Order in Council, the PCC may serve notice on the district council requiring them to maintain the churchyard. They in turn may pass the responsibility to a parish council, so be sure to think it through before acting, as responsibility may return to your local community.[27] Remember also that the local council will only maintain it to the standard they already keep other churchyards in the area, so have a look around the district. The council is still

---

26 Burial according to the rites of the Church of England should take place in consecrated ground which will be the final resting place of the deceased. A back garden does not fulfil either obligation. For private burial grounds and 'green burials' see *Legal Opinions concerning the Church of England*, p. 260.

27 Local Government Act 1972, s215.

subject to faculty jurisdiction for any work it carries out in the churchyard.

It is said that suicides can't be buried in a churchyard. Is this true?

No, it is not. However, caution is commended when it is suggested that someone has taken their own life. This is a complex pastoral question. It is for a coroner to decide if someone committed suicide, not a minister. Often, in such tragic circumstances, no such decision will have been concluded by the coroner at the time of the funeral. It may be wise to avoid the use of the term 'suicide' altogether. The general attitude towards suicide is very different today from times past.

The canons state that the duty to bury according to the usual rites of the Church of England does not extend to suicides, and that the minister should use such service as may be prescribed or approved by the bishop.[28] The funeral service in *Common Worship: Pastoral Services* does include, in the additional resources, prayers for use after a suicide, and it is thought that generally, unless a diocesan bishop has directed otherwise, it would be lawful to use the *Common Worship* service. It is not lawful to use the Book of Common Prayer in such circumstances.[29]

What happens when ...

... a deceased person does not have a right to burial?

No person, other than those with the right to burial, may be buried in the churchyard or burial ground without the consent of the minister of the parish. Where there is plenty of space it may be possible for the incumbent, probably in consultation with the PCC, to allow such burials where there is an appropriate reason to do so. When space is short it will probably not be appropriate, so that the limited space is available to those who have a right to burial.

---

28 Canon B38(2).
29 See also *Legal Opinions concerning the Church of England*, p. 69.

... someone asks for no Christian content in the service?

This requires a careful discussion with the family before a minister leaps in with a response. Families will often start by asking for 'no religion' but then go on to want readings and hymns! If they really do not want any religious content then it is not appropriate for a Church of England minister to take the service, since they are only authorized to take services according to the rites of the Church of England.[30] The minister should then advise the family to request the undertaker to find someone else to take the service.

... someone wants to exhume and re-inter a body?

This is a situation which is faced more often than you may think. In our mobile society people sometimes ask whether they can move a body or ashes from one churchyard to another. Exhumation and re-interment may be requested for a range of reasons. The principle of Christian burial is that it involves laying someone in their final resting place. There is, therefore, a very strong assumption against movement of remains after burial. Any such exhumation would require a faculty. The chancellors of the various dioceses have been fairly consistent about this and it is important to get advice if you are faced with any such request.[31]

... a memorial becomes dangerous?

When a burial takes place the ground remains the property of the PCC. Maintenance of the ground is the PCC's responsibility (see above). Any stone placed over the grave, by faculty permission, remains the property of the next of kin of the deceased. They would be responsible for its maintenance. This is not always helpful, as there may be no way of contacting them. In the case where a PCC finds that a stone or memorial is unsafe it should

---

30 Canon B2.
31 *Legal Opinions concerning the Church of England*, p. 251.

be laid flat immediately, to prevent injury or damage.[32] Where possible the registry should be contacted first for advice. Investigations can then begin to trace the owners of the memorial. A faculty should be sought to regulate matters as soon as possible. For closed churchyards the process would be handled by the local authority. If in doubt contact the diocesan registry.[33]

Resources you should have at your fingertips

- Canon B38.

- Canon F11.

- Your parish administration system and forms.

- The funeral services and other material are available in *Common Worship: Pastoral Services* available as a download from www.cofe.anglican.org/worship/liturgy/commonworship/texts/index.html

- You need to know the diocesan churchyard regulations which will be in the document in which the chancellor delegates authority to incumbents. Copies should be available in the diocesan handbook or from the Diocesan Advisory Committee (DAC) secretary.

- Some dioceses issue a Diocesan Churchyards Handbook and if there is one you should have a copy.

Useful links

- There is a lot of useful material on the theme of death and dying at www.crusebereavementcare.org.uk

- Information about hospice care in the UK is available at www.hospiceinformation.info

---

32 Occupiers Liability Act 1957.
33 *Legal Opinions concerning the Church of England*, p. 229.

- Your local undertakers are always a good local link. Get to know them and establish a good working relationship with them. There are two large professional bodies for undertakers, as well as a number of smaller groups.

- The National Association of Funeral Directors
  618 Warwick Road
  Solihull
  West Midlands
  B91 1AA
  Telephone: 0845 230 1343
  www.nafd.org.uk

- Society of Allied & Independent Funeral Directors
  Sawbridgeworth
  Herts CM21 9DB
  Telephone: 0845 230 6777
  www.saif.org.uk

- Funeral services in *Common Worship: Pastoral Services* are available for download from www.cofe.anglican.org/worship/liturgy/commonworship/texts/index.html

- The Joint Churches Group on Funeral Services at Cemeteries and Crematoria considers matters relating to funeral services in cemeteries and crematoria, liaises with funeral directors and others, publishes the *Joint Churches Service Book* for use in such places and reports and advises government through the Churches Main Committee: www.cmainc.org.uk

- Information about registration of a death can be found at www.gro.gov.uk

- Information about death benefits and other rights and responsibilities at the time of death can be found at www.direct.gov.uk/en/RightsAndResponsibilities/index.htm

- Memorials in churchyards tend to be very similar. If a distinctive memorial is desired, subject to faculty, then Memorials by Artists is a web-site which may be useful: www.memorialsby-artists.co.uk

9

Clergy

A possible scenario

Your new curate is due in a few months' time and some of you meet him on a visit to the parish from college. He clearly has fire in his belly, but that may be due to his Australian background. In the course of the conversation he happens to mention that he has no time or respect for either the bishop or the Queen, and would rather not swear allegiance to either! Where does he stand?

What you need to know

Orders in the Church of England

In the Church of England there are three orders of ministry, known as bishops, priests, and deacons. No one can be a bishop, priest, or deacon unless they have been called, tried, examined, and admitted according to the Ordinal.[1] It is normative that women can be ordained as priest or deacon in the Church of England,[2] although there are provisions for those who find this difficult to accept.[3]

---

1 Canon C1(1).
2 Canons C4A and C4B.
3 Priests (Ordination of Women) Measure 1993 which includes Resolutions A and B (See Chapter 10 for texts). The Episcopal Ministry Act of Synod 1993 provides for additional episcopal oversight. The resolution to be passed under this Act of Synod is sometimes referred to as Resolution C, although that is not a term used in the Act.

Who may be ordained?

To be ordained, a person must be baptized and confirmed. They must be sufficiently trained, which the canons state should include training in Scripture, and in the doctrine, discipline, and worship of the Church of England. Their lifestyle must be of good repute and such as to be an example to the church.[4] A person must also be reasonably healthy so as to be able to exercise their ministry.[5] There are specific provisions as to those who have been divorced or are married to someone who has been divorced.[6]

A person must usually be over 24 to be ordained priest.[7] Ordinations are arranged and conducted by the bishop.[8] Any other priests taking part in an ordination service join with the bishop by laying their hands on the head of a person who is being ordained priest.[9]

A person can only be ordained if they have some ecclesiastical office within which to exercise their ministry. This usually means that a deacon or priest must be ordained to a parish, although there is specific provision for a person holding office in a university, a master in a school, a person who is to be a chaplain in a university or college or school, a person who is to be a member of the staff of a theological college, and a person who is living under vows in the house of any religious order or community.[10]

A person to be ordained deacon must produce to the bishop a birth certificate and any references the bishop asks for.[11] A person who is to be ordained priest must produce to the bishop his or her Letters of Orders[12] and references.[13]

---

4 Canon C4(1).
5 Canon C4(2).
6 Canons C4(3) and C4(3A).
7 Canon C3(6).
8 Canon C3(1).
9 Canon C3(4).
10 Canon C5.
11 Canon C6(1).
12 The document given to someone when they are made a deacon.
13 Canon C6(2).

Where may someone minister?

Ministers may not exercise their ministry simply by virtue of being ordained. The ordination is what gives them the general authority to be a minister of the church. It is then the bishop's licence which gives them specific authority to exercise that ministry in a particular place. Ministers may not exercise their ministry without a licence or permission to officiate (PTO) from the bishop. The licence or PTO will specify where the ministry is to take place. Ministers may not exercise their ministry outside the area or parish to which they are licensed except with the permission of the minister of the other parish. There is an exception that allows ministry at the homes of those whose names are entered on their electoral roll.[14] Also, a minister may be permitted by the minister having the cure of souls to exercise their ministry in a parish for not more than seven days in three months without reference to the bishop.[15]

Oaths

Everyone who is to be ordained priest or deacon must first, in the presence of the ordaining bishop, take the Oath of Allegiance and the Oath of Canonical Obedience in the following words:

> I, *A B*, do swear that I will be faithful and bear true allegiance to Her Majesty Queen Elizabeth II, her heirs and successors, according to law: So help me God.[16]

> I, *A B*, do swear by Almighty God that I will pay true and canonical obedience to the Lord Bishop of *C* and his successors in all things lawful and honest: So help me God.[17]

Every person who is to be ordained priest or deacon must before ordination make the Declaration of Assent in the presence of the

---

14 Canon C8(4).
15 Canon C8(2)(a).
16 Canon C13.
17 Canon C14.

bishop. The preface which precedes the Declaration of Assent is said by the bishop.

PREFACE

The Church of England is part of the One, Holy, Catholic and Apostolic Church worshipping the one true God, Father, Son and Holy Spirit. It professes the faith uniquely revealed in the Holy Scriptures and set forth in the catholic creeds, which faith the Church is called upon to proclaim afresh in each generation. Led by the Holy Spirit, it has borne witness to Christian truth in its historic formularies, the Thirty-nine Articles of Religion, The Book of Common Prayer and the Ordering of Bishops, Priests and Deacons. In the declaration you are about to make will you affirm your loyalty to this inheritance of faith as your inspiration and guidance under God in bringing the grace and truth of Christ to this generation and making him known to those in your care?

Declaration of Assent

I, *A B*, do so affirm, and accordingly declare my belief in the faith which is revealed in the Holy Scriptures and set forth in the catholic creeds and to which the historic formularies of the Church of England bear witness; and in public prayer and administration of the sacraments, I will use only the forms of service which are authorized or allowed by canon.[18]

When someone is ordained, instituted or licensed in a place other than the place where they are to serve they must, on the first Sunday in their new parish, publicly read the Declaration of Assent. The Preface should be read by the incumbent (in the case of a curate) or a churchwarden (in the case of an incumbent) before the minister makes the Declaration.[19]

Lifestyle

Every bishop, priest, and deacon is under obligation to say Morning and Evening Prayer daily, either privately or openly, and to

---

18 Canon C15(1).
19 Canon C15(4).

celebrate the Holy Communion, or to be present, on all Sundays and other principal Feast Days. They are also to be conscientious in daily prayer and intercession, in personal reflection, in the study of the Scriptures, and in such other studies as are appropriate to their ministerial duties.[20]

Ministers are required to lead an appropriate lifestyle. They must live in a way which befits their calling and is not detrimental to the performance of the duties of their office. They must not cause offence to others. At all times they must fashion their lifestyle and that of their family according to the doctrine of Christ, and make themselves and their families wholesome examples to the church.[21] This is a high calling. There is also a range of guidance as to conduct in the recent *Guidelines for the Professional Conduct of Clergy*.

A minister holding ecclesiastical office may not engage in any other trade or any other occupation without the authority of the bishop.[22] The bishop has power to grant such permission to a minister to take on other work or occupations, but only after consultation with the PCC of the parish.[23]

Clerical dress

The style of dress of clergy has changed and developed over the centuries. In today's world the issue can be seen to be one on which clergy reach a wide range of conclusions. So far as the canons are concerned, the dress of a bishop, priest, or deacon must be suitable to their office and, save for purposes of recreation and other justifiable reasons, must be a sign and mark of their holy calling and ministry.[24] This is fine so far as it goes, but it does not really settle the matter. It probably allows sufficient leeway for clerical dress to continue to develop as it has over the years. Vesture for services is dealt with specifically by canon.[25]

---

20 Canon C26(1).
21 Canon C26(2).
22 Canon C28(1).
23 Canon C28(2).
24 Canon C27.
25 Canon B8 and see Chapter 15.

Confidentiality

One key issue which clergy need to have in mind is confidentiality. Clergy owe a duty of confidentiality to those they encounter pastorally. A person seeking pastoral guidance and counsel from the clergy has the right to expect that the clergyperson concerned will not pass on to a third party confidential information so obtained, without their consent or other lawful authority.[26] The content and process of a pastoral relationship may need to be shared with certain other people, such as a supervisor or supervisory group, consultant or other involved colleagues. Such sharing needs to be carefully restricted so that it does not involve any breach of confidence. Should it be desirable to discuss the relationship in such a way as to involve a breach of confidentiality, the consent of the person seeking pastoral guidance must first be obtained.[27]

The clergy should be aware of the circumstances in which confidential information can or should be disclosed to third parties, particularly where the safety of children is concerned.[28] If contemplating such a disclosure the clergy should seek appropriate legal and other specialist advice.[29] Special considerations apply where information is disclosed in the context of formal confession.[30]

FAQs

What does the oath of canonical obedience mean?

Clergy of the Church of England owe a duty of canonical obedience to the bishop in all things lawful and honest.[31] The meaning of these oaths is quite clear on the surface, although there is much debate as to the finer meanings of the words 'lawful' and 'honest'. It has been held that the duty only extends to obedience of an

---

26 *Guidelines for the Professional Conduct of Clergy*, para. 3.11.

27 *Guidelines for the Professional Conduct of Clergy*, para. 3.13.

28 See Chapter 20.

29 *Guidelines for the Professional Conduct of Clergy*, para. 3.14.

30 There is a fuller discussion as to the legal nature of confidentiality in *Legal Opinions concerning the Church of England*, p. 43ff.

31 Canon C1(3).

episcopal direction which is expressly authorized in law.[32] This is not a very broad interpretation of the spirit of the oaths, but it represents the legal position. The Privy Council said, in 1863: 'the oath of canonical obedience does not mean that every clergyman will obey all the commands of the bishop against which there is no law, but that he will obey all such commands as the bishop is authorized by law to impose'.[33]

Do clergy have to take them?

Yes. All clergy have to take the oaths at ordination and as they begin each new post in their ministry. They may affirm rather than swear[34] but the effect will be the same. This includes overseas clergy, who will owe the same duty to the Queen and the bishop while they are serving in this country.[35]

Can a minister join a union?

Yes, there is no reason why not. Most clergy do not see it as necessary but the Amicus Union has a section specializing in 'faith workers' and has begun to build some expertise in the area of 'employment' of faith workers. Their web-site details are below.

When a new minister arrives, what is the difference between licensing, institution, collation, induction and installation?

The bishop's part in the service welcoming a new minister is called *institution*, *collation* or *licensing*. If the parish priest is to be incumbent (rector or vicar) then the bishop either institutes or collates. They are the same thing, but the name changes to collation in the case when the bishop is also patron of the parish. If

---

32 Doe suggests the direction must be 'expressly or impliedly authorized by law, and ... not *ultra vires*'. *Legal Framework of the Church of England*, p. 214.

33 *Long v Bishop of Cape Town*, (1863) 1 Moo PCCNS 411 at 465.

34 Oaths Act 1978, s5.

35 *Legal Opinions concerning the Church of England*, p. 58.

the priest is to be a team vicar or a priest-in-charge then the name becomes licensing. In each case the priest is given a share in the bishop's cure (care) of souls.

After a priest has been collated or instituted, the bishop invites the archdeacon to *induct* the priest into the 'possession' of the benefice(s). In this short ceremony, the priest is in effect given a church building and a home to help in the task given by the bishop. In all cases the archdeacon then also *installs* (seats) the new priest.

What are OLMs and SSMs?

SSM stands for Self-Supporting Minister. The term used to be Non-Stipendiary Minister (NSM) but the terminology has changed several times and the Church of England has still not really found a term to describe such ministers which satisfies everyone. SSM seems to be the current preferred term. The only distinction is that such ministers have agreed at the time of selection and licensing that they will not receive payment for their ministry. In all other ways they are priests or deacons without distinction.

OLM stands for Ordained Local Minister. Several dioceses established OLM schemes during the 1990s. OLMs are priests or deacons, who should always be part of a local ministry team, and who agree at the time of their ordination that they will only minister in the local benefice in which they were ordained. In our mobile world, this has been found to bring certain difficulties and some dioceses have changed all such ministers' licences to SSM status.

What is the difference between a rector and a vicar?

There may be no other organization as proficient at causing confusion over names and titles as the Church of England! Priest, minister, rector, vicar, curate and padre are just the polite things I have been called from time to time. Each has its roots in a different place and ultimately they make no difference to how God sees us!

The terms 'priest' and 'minister' tend to be descriptive of the simple fact that the person is an authorized minister of the church. 'Rector', 'vicar' and 'curate' are all descriptions of the roles clergy are given. 'Rector' and 'vicar' are the two terms used of incumbents: those instituted as the holder of the office in a benefice.[36] Historically there was a difference, but there is none today. Curates are their assistants. When the benefice is suspended[37] the minister working in the parish in exactly the same way as a rector or vicar is technically called a priest in charge, although most locals who know nothing of church law will think of them as rector or vicar. 'Padre' tends to be used by those who have some military background as it is the usual term of address in the forces.

What happens when ...

... a minister wants to resign from a post?

Holy Orders are by nature lifelong. However, a minister may wish to relinquish his or her ministry in a particular post or to cease to minister in the church, and this can be done by signing a deed to that effect. The diocesan registry would draw up such a deed.

... clergy wish to retire?

Clergy must retire at the age of 70.[38] There is a provision allowing the bishop to extend this by up to two years with the consent of the relevant PCC.[39] Clergy may retire earlier, and the issue is then usually one to do with the level of pension. The earliest point at which a full pension could be available would be 65.[40] Full

---

36 This term historically referred to the benefits or income received by a priest from the parish (glebe income, tithes etc.). It now refers to the unit of legal ecclesiastical organization to which a minister is appointed, and can be a parish, a group of parishes or a team.

37 See Chapter 10.

38 Ecclesiastical Offices (Age Limit) Measure 1975, s1.

39 Ecclesiastical Offices (Age Limit) Measure 1975, s3.

40 Proposals before General Synod may raise this age slightly in the future.

information on pension matters can be obtained from the Church of England Pensions Board. It is possible for the bishop, after proper enquiry and due process, to seek to force an incumbent to retire when he or she is unable, by reason of age or infirmity of mind or body, to discharge duties adequately.[41] It is rarely used because it is complex and costly, and the new terms of service provisions currently before General Synod may make this process obsolete.

... there is pastoral breakdown in a parish?

It is a matter of great sadness and strain when relationships between a minister and a parish break down. It is rarely possible to make swift decisions as to where blame lies as relationship matters can be very complex. When this breakdown is such as to impede the mission of the church[42] there is provision for an inquiry to take place and for the bishop to take action.[43] A request for an inquiry into the situation may be made by the incumbent, the archdeacon or by two-thirds of the PCC.[44] After the request is first made there must be a period of between six and twelve months while attempts at reconciliation are made. The archdeacon conducts a preliminary investigation to establish whether a formal inquiry should take place, and if appropriate the full inquiry is then instituted by the diocesan secretary. The proceedings are conducted by a five-member panel including a chancellor, two clergy and two lay members, all of whom will be from outside the diocese.[45] The tribunal reports to the bishop and makes recommendations as to what action should be taken.[46] The bishop then has power to remove or rebuke the minister or to disqualify lay people from holding office for a period of up to five years or rebuke them. The bishop may also give pastoral guidance.[47] Ultimately none

---

41 Incumbent (Vacation of Benefices) Measure 1977, s6.
42 Incumbent (Vacation of Benefices) Measure 1977, s19A.
43 Incumbent (Vacation of Benefices) Measure 1977, s1A.
44 Incumbent (Vacation of Benefices) Measure 1977, s1A.
45 Incumbent (Vacation of Benefices) Measure 1977, s5 & 7.
46 Incumbent (Vacation of Benefices) Measure 1977, s9.
47 Incumbent (Vacation of Benefices) Measure 1977, s10.

of this will restore the relationships in a Christian manner, but sometimes it is necessary where things have gone wrong. Where matters are of a disciplinary nature, rather than a pastoral break-down, the procedure is different.[48]

Resources you should have at your fingertips

- Canon C1.3.

- Canons C13–C15.

- *Guidelines for the Professional Conduct of Clergy.*

Useful links

- The union which has a branch specializing in faith workers, including clergy of the Church of England, is Amicus. Their faith-worker section can be found through the main web-site at www.amicustheunion.org

- *Guidelines for the Professional Conduct of Clergy* is available from the Church of England web-site: www.cofe.anglican.org/lifeevents/ministry/profcond.pdf

---

48 See Chapter 11.

10

Appointments

A possible scenario

You are coming towards the end of your curacy. Fortunately, your vicar has been ordained for decades and knows how things work and is able to advise you. 'Don't worry, old boy. It's just a matter of trust. Let the bishop know what sort of thing you are looking for and he'll sort something out for you.' Is this good advice?

What you need to know

A *changing culture*

The days when the bishop sent a priest to work in the parish are long gone, if they ever existed. The appointment process, specifically to incumbency posts in the Church of England, is more and more reflecting the language and methods of the human resources department of a company. We may spend much time discussing whether this is a good thing, but if clergy want a new post, that is the world they will probably have to enter. The appointment process is regulated by canon[1] and by measure.[2]

It is helpful towards understanding the appointment system to know that a lot of the process happens in an informal way in current practice in the Church of England. Parishes are often consulted fully by the diocese or patron before the formal process begins, and the interviewing at the heart of the process is not legislated for in the measure at all, and can be done in a range of ways. When you add to this the fact that the formal process also

---

1 Canon C9(1).
2 Patronage (Benefices) Measure 1986.

has to be followed in parallel with this informal practice, it is no wonder many clergy and parish representatives (and, dare I say it, bishops and archdeacons) end up confused by the system.

The three parties involved in an appointment

There are three parties who are involved in an appointment to an incumbency. Their respective roles have been described as like the legs of a tripod, bringing stability to the process.[3] The patron of a parish *nominates* a candidate. The PCC, through its elected representatives, *affirms* the patron's nomination. The bishop then *institutes* the person to their new ministry. It can immediately be seen that the bishop's role is not as significant as many would lead you to believe. However, what is clear is that all three parties need to play their distinctive parts, so that together they can make an appointment to the benefice.

Getting started

When a vacancy occurs in a parish the formal process begins when the bishop gives notice to the diocese's 'designated officer'.[4] The designated officer then informs the registered patron(s).[5] Patrons are required to state who is to act on their behalf in the vacancy and that he or she is a communicant member of the Church of England.[6] The designated officer also notifies the secretary of the PCC(s). It (or they) must meet within 28 days to discuss and decide six matters which the notice of vacancy specifies. In the case of multi-parish benefices the PCCs have to meet together to take these decisions.[7] This is known as the 'section 11 meeting', and is one of the key things a PCC must do.

It is quite possible that a vacancy will come as no surprise to anyone in the parish. If the priest has left to move to another post, or has retired, the PCC may have had some considerable time to

---

3 Parrott and Field, *Situation Vacant*, p. 4.
4 Usually the registrar or pastoral secretary of the diocese.
5 Patronage (Benefices) Measure 1986, s7.
6 Patronage (Benefices) Measure 1986, s8.
7 Patronage (Benefices) Measure 1986, s11.

prepare. If the vacancy arises due to a death the time may be less, but it is still possible for the PCC to have had a range of discussions, and even have had meetings with the bishop, archdeacon and patron informally before the formal notice of vacancy activates the process, and its strict timetable.

Section 11 meetings

The section 11 meeting must consider six issues and should not have any other business to discuss. These are:

1 Prepare a statement describing the conditions, needs and traditions of the parish.

This is a crucial document. As well as the essential factual information, it should contain the PCC's estimate of the qualities and skills required in the next vicar or rector. Many dioceses provide guidelines or a *pro forma* to help PCCs in this task. Once completed, copies of the statement must be sent, within strict time limits, to both patron and bishop. If more than one parish is involved, a joint statement may be produced. Alternatively, different parishes may make separate statements – in which case a co-ordinating addendum is very helpful. This is not a task which can be achieved in a single meeting (as the measure acknowledges) so it may be wise to delegate drafting to a small group.

2 Appoint two lay members to represent the PCC in the process.

They may, but need not, be the churchwardens. It is these representatives who have the power to approve the patron's nominee. When more than one PCC is involved each council has the right to elect at least one member to represent it. The code of practice issued in 1989 suggests the following pattern:

> *two parishes:* two representatives from each PCC
> *three parishes:* either two from each or two from one and one from each of the other two
> *four or more parishes:* one from each.

3 Decide whether to request the patron(s) to advertise the post.

The PCC cannot insist, and it may well be expected to foot the bill if the patron agrees.

4 Decide whether to ask for a meeting of bishop, patron and PCC to discuss the parish statement.

Any of the three parties may call for such a meeting under section 12 of the measure (therefore referred to as a 'section 12 meeting'). Bishops vary greatly in the way they use this right. Some call section 12 meetings as a matter of course, while others regard them as emergency fall-back devices only to be used when relationships are particularly fragile and misunderstandings likely. It is common practice in some dioceses to call an informal meeting early in the vacancy at which the bishop, archdeacon, rural dean and PCC sit down and discuss any issues concerning the vacancy and the process which is to be followed. In this case it is rarely necessary to call a formal section 12 meeting at a later stage in the process.

5 Decide whether to request a statement in writing from the bishop describing the needs of the diocese in relation to the benefice and the wider interests of the church.

Most PCCs feel this is an unnecessary step if the bishop or archdeacon is planning to visit them anyway, or has already done so, to discuss the vacancy. If, however, the bishop expects the incumbent of a small benefice to take on additional diocesan duties it may help the PCC and patron to have some firm information about the level of commitment involved.

6 Consider two formal resolutions arising from the Priests (Ordination of Women) Measure 1993. These are:

Resolution A That this PCC would not accept a woman as the minister who presides at or celebrates Holy Communion or pronounces Absolution in this parish.

Resolution B That this PCC would not accept a woman as incumbent or priest-in-charge of the benefice or as a team vicar in the benefice.

The PCC is not required to vote on either resolution if it does not want to, but it is required to decide whether to vote or not. Its representatives are open to prosecution if they veto the appointment of a woman (on gender grounds alone) when Resolution B has not been passed.[8]

It is the PCC's responsibility, then, to take these important steps in preparing the process for appointing a new vicar or rector. Inevitably, it takes time and effort to do all these things well. So much the better, therefore, if the outgoing incumbent can give the PCC a little notice of his or her intention to go, so that it can push ahead with its preparations before the measure's deadlines become operative. This is particularly valuable for multi-parish benefices where timetabling meetings and setting up the necessary structures for liaison may be time-consuming.

Gathering names

This is the patron's primary contribution to the process. In whatever way patronage is expressed (through an individual, a group, a trust or a board) the initial aim is to find a number of ordained men and women (unless the PCC has passed Resolution B) who most closely match the situation, tasks and needs identified by the parish statement. The measure is completely silent as to how this will happen. It may seem like a mysterious process on some occasions, and on others it is all very open and collaborative, with the bishop, patron and parish representatives all involved together.[9] Some patrons will take up the parish's suggestion of advertising, and may do so in the church press. Others will use their own networks and contacts to find appropriate candidates.

---

8 A PCC cannot consider Resolution C at the time of a vacancy, as it requires the minister to consent and no minister is in place at that time.

9 For a full discussion of the possible models see Parrott and Field, *Situation Vacant*, pp. 9–10.

Approving the candidate

Legally, this is the prerogative of the elected PCC representatives. Indeed, their only formal role is to decide whether or not they wish to approve the patron's nomination.[10] Some patrons will seek to involve them much more than that but the representatives can only take a fuller part in the process if the patron invites them to do so. They will, of course, have a perfectly legitimate concern to maximize their information about any candidate before deciding whether or not to approve him or her. Some patrons will provide plenty of paperwork in advance of the candidate's visit, but others will not. There are various options open to the PCC representatives at this point. They may seek the views of others, but they must remember that the final decision is theirs and theirs alone.[11]

If they decide to veto the patron's nominee, and the patron does not appeal against their decision to the archbishop, the process simply moves back a step and the patron puts forward another candidate.

Completing the appointment

It is at this stage that the process can seem confusing. If an interview model has been involved, and the patron, bishop and parish representatives have all agreed on a candidate it may look as though the process has stepped backwards. This is because that interview process was part of the patron's informal method of gathering names. Once a name has emerged the formal parts of the process reassert themselves.

Both the PCC representatives and the bishop have to sign legal documents accepting the patron's nomination.[12] If the bishop has not been brought into the process before this stage, he will almost certainly want to interview the chosen candidate himself before signing on the dotted line.

Once the documents have been signed the patron can formally

---

10 Patronage (Benefices) Measure 1986, s13.
11 See Parrott and Field, *Situation Vacant*, pp. 21–2.
12 Patronage (Benefices) Measure 1986, s13.

offer the benefice to the priest. The priest must reply accepting the post. The patron then gives notice of presentation to the bishop. It is only at this point that a public announcement can be made – preferably in both the candidate's and the 'receiving' church on the same Sunday – and a date fixed for the new incumbent's arrival in the parish.

Even at this stage, when the date of the institution (or collation) has been fixed, the legalities are not quite complete. The bishop must give formal notice to the designated officer, the registrar, the patron, the archdeacon, the rural dean and the incumbent-to-be. The registrar then notifies the PCC secretary, who is instructed to post a notice on the church door for a fortnight announcing the bishop's intention to institute a new incumbent. Only when this notice has been sent back to the registrar with the PCC secretary's endorsement can the institution proceed.

FAQs

What does suspension mean?

Everything written so far assumes that the process, set in place by the measure of 1986, is allowed to take its course without a hitch. There are situations, however, in which the bishop is entitled to build a delay into the system.[13] With the consent of the Diocesan Pastoral Committee, he is allowed to *suspend* the patron's right to present a nominee for a vacant benefice in certain circumstances for a maximum period of five years.[14] Before doing so he must consult all the interested parties. This may be done for a number of reasons. First, and most often, he may suspend the process of appointing an incumbent while a pastoral scheme affecting the benefice passes through its various consultative stages. Such a scheme often involves joining two or more benefices into a group, a team or a new united benefice. Second, suspension is allowed when the bishop wants to change the parsonage house of a benefice. Third, suspensions sometimes occur when an

---

13 Pastoral Measure 1983, ss67 and 69.
14 Pastoral Measure 1983, s67.

incoming parish priest will be required to take on additional diocesan responsibilities.

Further, the bishop may *restrict* the patron's right to present for a period of one year, where pastoral reorganization is *already* under formal discussion. The main distinction here is that this can be done without consultation, but only for the shorter period.[15]

Suspension or restriction of the patron's right to present does not mean that the parish cannot have a minister. Instead of a vicar or rector the bishop may appoint a priest-in-charge. The latter is licensed for a period, not instituted with a freehold, but he or she is usually accepted by the parish as 'the vicar'. The difference in the appointment of a priest-in-charge is that the bishop is not bound to accept the patron's suggestions or to respect the PCCs objections. In practice many bishops follow the same procedure, even though they are not bound to do so.

None of this sounds familiar – isn't it just an interview system now?

It can sound confusing, not least because the legal process is built a bit like a Polo-mint. There is a hole in the middle at the point when selection of candidates take place, leaving a range of options open to patrons. It is certainly not as simple as a secular interview and appointment process but if you have read and understood what I have said above then you should find your way through the process and understand what is happening whether you are a candidate, bishop, patron or a parish representative.

When does a vacancy formally start?

The vacancy starts when the outgoing minister either retires, dies, signs a deed of resignation or is formally instituted into his or her next job. Note, however, that the timetables referred to start from the date of issue of the notice of vacancy to the PCC secretary.

---

15 Pastoral Measure 1983, s69.

What happens when ...

... *someone changes their mind*

So far as the bishop, patron or parish representatives are concerned they have made their final decision at the moment they sign off the various forms accepting the candidate. So far as the minister is concerned they may, in theory, change their mind at any time up to the moment they are instituted or licensed. It does not often happen, but occasionally something happens which means that a candidate withdraws.

... *the new minister is welcomed to the parish?*

There is usually a service of welcome which takes various titles. This service is usually in a form approved by the bishop for use in the diocese. In the service the bishop and the archdeacon formally institute the new ministry and the parish welcomes their new minister. This service is usually organized by the rural dean under the direction of the bishop.[16]

... *things drag on?*

The patron has nine months from the time of the notice of vacancy to complete all the formal stages of the process.[17] If that time passes the right of the patron lapses and passes to the archbishop of the province. The task of finding a new priest continues, and often the patron is consulted, but ultimately the responsibility rests with the archbishop rather than the patron.

Resources you should have at your fingertips

• Patronage (Benefices) Measure 1986.

• David Parrott and David Field, *Situation Vacant: A Guide to*

---

16 For definitions of the various technical terms used in this service see Chapter 9.

17 Patronage (Benefices) Measure 1986, s16.

the Appointment Process in the Church of England, Cambridge, Grove Books Pastoral 65, 2005.

Useful links

- The Archbishops' Clergy Appointments Adviser has a web-site at www.cofe.anglican.org/info/caa. This includes a guide to the process at www.cofe.anglican.org/info/caa/goodpractice.doc

- Private Patrons Consultative Group, part of the English Clergy Association, also publish a guide to the process. This can be found at http://www.clergyassoc.co.uk/content/privatepatrons.htm

- The Church Pastoral Aid Society (CPAS) has a patronage department and their web-site contains lots of useful advice and downloads: www.cpas.org.uk/patronage/content/

- The church papers are another obvious point for looking for a job. The job advertisements can be seen on-line as well at www.churchtimes.co.uk and www.churchnewspaper.com

11

Clergy Discipline

A possible scenario

You find your rector a very difficult person. Everything he says or does seems to wind you up and relationships are becoming very difficult, not just for you but for the whole PCC. Several people have discussed whether to write to the bishop, but have not done so to date. A friend tells you that there is a new piece of church law, which will mean that you can get rid of the rector. Is this so?

What you need to know

Generally

The whole way in which clergy understand their role and the expectations of others upon them has changed and goes on changing. The Clergy Discipline Measure 2003 (CDM) creates formal disciplinary procedures against clergy who commit ecclesiastical offences. Further, the General Synod is working on the draft Ecclesiastical Offices (Terms of Service) Measure which will add to the disciplinary procedure a competency procedure. This latter measure is not yet in force, and final details have still to be approved but this chapter will set out the provisions of the CDM and look briefly at the possible effects of the Terms of Service Measure.

Clergy Discipline Measure 2003

This measure provides a structure for dealing efficiently and fairly with formal complaints of misconduct against members of the clergy (except in relation to matters involving doctrine, ritual or ceremonial[1]). All admitted to Holy Orders in the Church of England are covered by the measure, whether or not they are in active ministry. Where the formal complaint concerns priests or deacons, the disciplinary structure is centred on the bishop.[2]

Grounds for a complaint

There are four grounds for alleging misconduct, namely:

- Acting in breach of ecclesiastical law.
- Failing to do something which should have been done under ecclesiastical law.
- Neglecting to perform or being inefficient in performing the duties of office.
- Engaging in conduct that is unbecoming or inappropriate to the office and work of the clergy.[3]

The complaint procedure

The disciplinary process is started by a formal written complaint, which is made to the bishop. The complainant must produce written evidence in support of the complaint, and verify the complaint by a statement of truth.[4] The complaint and the evidence in support are referred by the bishop to the diocesan registrar for advice on whether the complainant is entitled to make the complaint, and whether the allegations are of sufficient substance to justify proceeding with it under the measure. This is the 'preliminary scrutiny' stage.[5]

Having received the registrar's advice, if the bishop considers that the complainant is entitled to complain and that the complaint deserves further consideration, he will invite the priest or

---

1 Complaints about these matters will still be dealt with under the Ecclesiastical Jurisdiction Measure 1963.

2 Clergy Discipline Measure 2003, s8.

3 Clergy Discipline Measure 2003, s.8(1).

4 Clergy Discipline Measure 2003, s10 and Clergy Discipline Rules, rule 4.

5 Clergy Discipline Measure 2003, s11.

deacon about whom the complaint is made ('the respondent'), to send a written answer verified by a statement of truth, together with evidence in support. The bishop will then decide the appropriate course to pursue. There are various ways the bishop can react at this stage:

- he may take no further action; or
- he may, if the respondent consents, direct that the matter remain on the record conditionally; or
- he may direct that an attempt be made to bring about conciliation; or
- he may impose a penalty by consent; or
- he may direct that the complaint is to be formally investigated.[6]

It is expected that the vast majority of cases will be dealt with by the bishop. In the minority of cases the designated officer (an officer appointed by the archbishop for this purpose) is asked to investigate the complaint. The designated officer will produce a report for the President of Tribunals, who will then decide if there is a case to answer before a bishop's disciplinary tribunal.[7] A tribunal will consist of two clergy and two lay people, plus an experienced lawyer in the chair.[8] If a complaint is proved, the tribunal can impose penalties.

One or more of the following penalties may be imposed on a respondent upon a finding that he has committed any misconduct, namely: permanent or limited prohibition (an order preventing a cleric from ministering), removal from office, revocation of a licence, an injunction or order to do or to refrain from doing a specified act, or a rebuke.[9]

Where a penalty is imposed under the measure, either by the bishop (with the consent of the respondent) or by the bishop's disciplinary tribunal, it will be recorded in the Archbishops' List, which will be maintained at Lambeth Palace. The respondent will

---

6 Clergy Discipline Measure 2003, s12.

7 Clergy Discipline Measure 2003, s17.

8 Clergy Discipline Measure 2003, s21.

9 Clergy Discipline Measure 2003, s24. It is broadly similar to that in Ecclesiastical Jurisdiction Measure 1963, s49.

be informed of the particulars to be recorded, and may request the President of Tribunals to review and alter the entry.[10]

Ecclesiastical Offices (Terms of Service) Measure

The Clergy Discipline Measure is still relatively new and it is only one half of what will be the new regime. The other part will be the Ecclesiastical Offices (Terms of Service) Measure. For the purposes of this chapter the important part of that draft measure will be the proposed competence procedure. The introduction to the draft procedure states: 'It is now recognized that for the minority who experience difficulties there should be a procedure for the Church to offer support and, where necessary, ultimately to consider whether these clergy are capable of holding office or of continuing in their present office. Although such cases will be rare, they can be damaging both to the minister concerned and to others affected.'[11] The details of the capability procedure are not yet finalized at the time of writing, and it would be unwise to set it out in detail until it is in force. However, clergy should note that it is one part of the 'Terms of Service' package which includes rights as well as responsibilities.

FAQs

Have I anything to fear?

Almost certainly not. The Clergy Discipline Measure is not there to create a culture of fear. Indeed the objective is described as to deal with the issues justly, in a way that is both fair to all relevant interested persons and proportionate to the nature and seriousness of the issues raised.[12] Most clergy will have absolutely nothing to fear from the new legislation, but it is hoped that the two measures and such documents as the *Guidelines for Professional*

---

10 Clergy Discipline Measure 2003, s38.

11 Ecclesiastical Offices (Terms of Service) Measure. Introduction to the Draft Procedure (ref. GS 1637-9X), p. 27.

12 Clergy Discipline Rules 2005, rule 1.

Conduct of Clergy will together increase the general level of professional practice among the church's ministers.

What happens when ...

... *we are not getting on with our vicar?*

The first advice is not to rush into any formal proceedings. Get the archdeacon involved and ask for help from others with skills in mediation. If all else fails, the Church of England web-site has a helpful leaflet explaining how the process works.

Resources you should have at your fingertips

- *Guidelines for the Professional Conduct of Clergy.*

Useful links

- *Guidelines for the Professional Conduct of Clergy* is available from the Church of England web-site: www.cofe.anglican.org/lifeevents/ministry/profcond.pdf

- Sometimes it might help clergy to have assistance in the matters described in this chapter. The Amicus Union has a branch specializing in faith-workers, including clergy of the Church of England. Their faith-worker section can be found through the main web-site at www.amicustheunion.org

- A leaflet explaining how the process works is available on the Church of England web-site at www.cofe.anglican.org/about/churchlawlegis/clergydiscipline/makingcomplaint.rtf

12

Reader Ministry

A possible scenario

A new minister has recently arrived in the parish where you have been a reader for many years. She wants you to have a work agreement. You have managed without one for the last 15 years and can't see why you need one now! You would rather just carry on doing the various things in the parish which have always been your job. After all, as a volunteer, you should be able to decide what you do, not her. Is this correct?

What you need to know

The office of a reader

Readers are men and women, from a wide range of occupations and backgrounds, who have been called by God and the church. They exercise an authorized voluntary ministry of preaching and teaching. They may also conduct worship, and assist in the pastoral, evangelistic and liturgical work of the church in the parish or area where they are licensed. As well as their formal roles readers have many informal ways of ministering by their presence, witness and listening at their places of work, at home, among the neighbours and in their local communities. They are often key lay leaders in their churches.

How readers are selected and trained

Each diocese has its own selection and training programme, but the office is recognized nationally, and the diocesan training is moderated to ensure a certain level of consistency. Candidates are nominated by their minister,[1] usually with the consent of the PCC. They must be baptized and confirmed,[2] regular communicants, have a good understanding of the faith and a good lifestyle.[3]

The training provided by each diocese must ensure that a reader has a good knowledge of Scripture and of the doctrine and worship of the Church of England, and that they are able to teach, preach and lead the services well.[4]

How readers are admitted

Following their training readers are admitted to office. Like ordination, this is something that happens just once. Unlike ordination, it does not include the laying on of hands, but the admission is signified by the giving of a New Testament.[5] The bishop gives the reader a certificate which may be presented to another bishop, if the reader moves to another diocese, as proof of admission.[6]

Declarations

Readers are not required to take oaths at their admission and at their licensing. Rather they make declarations. These are similar but not identical to the oaths clergy take. They must take the Declaration of Assent in exactly the same format as for clergy (with the appropriate adaptations to the Preface which is read by the bishop).[7] They must also make a Declaration of Obedience in the following form:

I, *A B*, will give due obedience to the Lord Bishop of *C* and his successors in all things lawful and honest.[8]

---

1 Canon E5(2).
2 Canon E4(1).
3 Canon E5(3).
4 Canon E5(3).
5 Canon E5(5).
6 Canon E5(6).
7 See Chapter 9 for the form of words. It is also in Canon E5(4).
8 Canon E5(4).

They must also make the following declaration:

> I, *A B*, about to be licensed to exercise the office of Reader in the parish of *C*, do hereby promise to endeavour, as far as in me lies, to promote peace and unity, and to conduct myself as becomes a worker for Christ, for the good of his Church, and for the spiritual welfare of all people. I will give due obedience to the minister in whose cure I may serve, in all things lawful and honest.[9]

Deployment

Practice varies between dioceses, but in many places one of the criteria for selection is a willingness to be deployed. Readers may, therefore, after their training be deployed either to their sending parish or elsewhere. It is very common for their first post to be their sending parish, and indeed part of the requirement of nomination is that the nominating minister describes the type of ministry which the potential reader may fulfil.[10] In appropriate circumstances readers may be seconded or redeployed to new areas of ministry.

If a reader moves home or decides to worship in another parish or place within the same diocese they should inform the Warden of Readers, and after a sufficient period, the incumbent should contact the Warden to ask that the reader's licence be transferred. There is no formal provision as to how long this period should be, but it is common to allow six months for a reader to settle into a new place before the decision is taken as to whether the reader should be licensed there.

Licensing

There is a distinction between admission and licensing. Admission is to the office of reader, and once admitted a reader remains in that office even if they are not exercising their ministry. No

---

9 Canon E6(2).
10 Canon E5(2).

reader may exercise their ministry without the bishop's licence.[11] Initially this is usually granted at admission, but if a move is made a new licence will be required.

A licence is usually until the age of 70[12] although it may be for a fixed period, in which case the reader will need to seek a renewal. The licence will authorize the reader to minister in their own diocese and indicate the area in which they may minister and the duties they are permitted to perform. Readers in active ministry over the age of 70 must hold the bishop's Permission to Officiate (PTO). Again this will indicate the area in which they may minister and the duties they are permitted to perform and should be for a limited period, subject to renewal, normally annually.

The duties of a reader

Readers may:

- Preach.
- Lead worship, except those services and parts of services specifically excluded by canon.
- Read the Old or New Testament readings, Epistle or Gospel at any service.
- Lead intercessions.
- Receive and present the offerings of the people.
- Distribute the consecrated bread and wine to the people.
- Take Communion to the sick and housebound.
- Publish banns of marriage in the absence of a priest.
- Undertake pastoral and educational work.
- Assist any minister as the bishop may direct.[13]

With permission from the incumbent of the parish, readers may:

- Accept occasional invitations to take part in services in a church of another denomination.

---

11 Canon E6(1).

12 Except in a team ministry where it may be for a term of years. Canon E6(1A).

13 Canon E4(2).

With permission from the bishop, readers may:

- Officiate at Communion by extension services.[14]
- Officiate at funeral services (with the good will of the persons responsible).[15]
- Accept regular invitations to take part in services in a church of another denomination, with the approval also of the PCC of the parish where the service is to take place.[16]

Readers may not:

- Officiate at baptism, except in an emergency situation when it is lawful for any lay person to baptize.[17]
- Officiate at a marriage service.[18]
- Pronounce the Absolution or give a Blessing but should use an authorized alternative form of words.[19]

Unless the licence prevents them from doing so, readers may minister in parishes in their locality, and indeed many rural areas rely on readers' ministry for their services. As a matter of courtesy readers should consult their incumbent before accepting engagements outside their own parish.

Dress

The normal dress of readers for liturgical duties is cassock, surplice, hood of degree (where appropriate) and plain blue scarf. A cassock alb may be worn at the Holy Communion if this is the custom of the parish.[20]

---

14 Depending on local diocesan regulations on this subject.
15 Canon E4(2A).
16 Canon B43(6).
17 See Chapter 6.
18 See Chapter 7.
19 Canon E4(2)(b).
20 From information document on the Church of England Readers web-site, www.readers.cofe.anglican.org, p. 23.

Ministry agreements

Readers should have a written agreement with their incumbent setting out the duties to be undertaken. There will probably be a diocesan template for this agreement. This should cover:

- the reader's particular gifts and ministry;
- the reader's role within the ministerial team;
- arrangements for Continuing Ministerial Education;
- attendance at reader meetings;
- arrangements for meetings between readers, clergy and other staff;
- the reader's role in relation to the PCC (see below);
- arrangements for reimbursement of expenses incurred through performance of reader duties;
- time off;
- work–life balance, between the reader role and the requirements of family, work and leisure.

This agreement should be reviewed regularly by the reader and incumbent together, normally once a year, and also at the time of the renewal of licence. Readers are normally voluntary and unpaid ministers but may be reimbursed for travelling and other expenses incurred through the performance of their duties. Expenses incurred through serving outside their normal parish should be reimbursed fully by the parish using the services of the reader.

Ministry review

Dioceses vary as to how the ministry of readers is reviewed, but good practice would be for them to have a regular pattern of review with someone other than their incumbent. Readers might keep a record of their ministry, services led, sermons preached, training attended and other ministry exercised. Subject to issues of confidentiality, a brief summary of a review should be placed in the reader's records.

Continuing ministerial education

Licensing is not the end of becoming a reader. To preach the word of God, readers must keep up their private reading and undertake ongoing training. Readers should be encouraged both by their incumbent and by the Warden of Readers to develop their ministry and understanding of the faith as the years go by. A commitment to continuing training is an essential part of a reader's life and ministry.

FAQs

Is a reader automatically on the PCC?

No. It is for the APCM to decide whether a reader (or readers) licensed in the parish should be on the PCC. This is often done according to the wishes of each reader, but ultimately no reader can insist on being on the PCC if the APCM decides otherwise.[21]

Can a reader be removed?

As described above, the admission of a reader is to an office, in which the person will remain. However, the bishop may revoke a reader's licence, without which he or she cannot minister. The revocation can be summary and for any cause which the bishop sees as good and reasonable. The reader must be given opportunity to show reason why the licence should not be revoked. There is a right of appeal to the archbishop.[22]

Can a reader receive a stipend?

Generally reader ministry is by nature a voluntary ministry. However, there is provision in the canons for a stipendiary licence, but the bishop must satisfy himself that provision has been made for

---

21 Church Representation Rules, rule 14(1)(e).
22 Canon E6(3).

the stipend to be paid, and for sickness and accident insurance and pension provision to be in place.[23]

What is a Warden of Readers?

Each diocese usually appoints someone, accountable to the bishop, to oversee the ministry of readers and to administer the network of readers in the diocese. This role is usually known as Warden of Readers, although there may be other titles in use in some places (such as Secretary of the Reader Committee).

What happens when ...

... a reader takes a funeral?

Readers can be authorized to take funerals, and many do. Strictly speaking the family should be asked for consent, but in places where I have worked the reader was simply seen as a member of the team taking funerals and no one ever quibbled. He explained that he was a lay minister, when he first spoke to the family, but such niceties are fairly meaningless to the bereaved, and rightly so. Indeed, most bereaved families described my reader as 'vicar' and, wisely, he did not waste time arguing. When readers conduct a funeral, they may not retain the fee. Fees collected should be passed to the incumbent or PCC treasurer, or in a vacancy to the Diocesan Board of Finance.

... there is a vacancy in the parish?

During a clergy vacancy the reader's ministry normally continues with supervision and support from the rural dean and churchwardens. The reader has no legal responsibilities for the parish, which fall usually to the churchwardens and the rural dean, but as the person who is leading and preaching during this crucial time they have an important part to play in leading the parish through a time of change.

---

23 Canon E6(4).

Good practice suggests that a potential incumbent should be made aware of any existing readers in the parish and it would be prudent to establish that an incoming incumbent would be willing to work with a reader who is already licensed to the parish.[24]

... a reader is invited to preach outside their own diocese?

Readers invited to conduct a service or to preach outside their own diocese should ask permission from the bishop of the diocese concerned, through the Warden of Readers of that diocese.

... a reader moves to another diocese?

When a reader moves to a new diocese they will need a new licence from the bishop of that diocese. It is the responsibility of a reader leaving a diocese to notify their Warden of Readers of their departure and new address, so that advice and help may be provided. (It is helpful to give the name of the new diocese if known, as different parts of some counties may be in different dioceses.) After settling into regular worship, the reader should approach the incumbent there and discuss whether there would be an appropriate role as reader.

Readers' Regulations vary from diocese to diocese. The Warden of Readers of the new diocese will be able to provide information about the length of time a reader needs to worship in a benefice before the incumbent and PCC may nominate the person for licensing, or whether the reader might be given temporary PTO by the bishop, or whether it is appropriate to be licensed to a deanery. They may be able to assist if the reader has difficulty finding a parish where their ministry would be welcomed.

Where an admitted reader seeks to be licensed in another diocese, references are usually taken up with the diocese where the person was previously licensed and proof of admission (usually the person's admission certificate) may be required.

---

24 See also Chapter 10.

Resources you should have at your fingertips

Diocesan Reader Regulations.

Useful links

Readers' web-site: www.readers.cofe.anglican.org

13

Rural Deans

A possible scenario

You are the rural dean. Rumour has it that the vicar of one of the parishes in the deanery is having an affair. Another openly claims that she has lost her faith, while a third has just rebuilt the church annex and carpeted the chancel but you are not sure whether they applied for a faculty. Can you or should you do anything?

What you need to know

Generally

The office of rural dean has ancient roots in the church but fell into disuse in the Middle Ages. In 1836 the role was revived by Act of Parliament[1] and became one mainly of inspection and reporting. The role is now regulated by canon.[2] The title 'rural dean' is outdated in many urban areas and the title 'area dean' is now authorized,[3] although for simplicity I shall use the term 'rural dean' throughout this chapter. The role continues to develop, change and grow and each diocese has its own regulations and expectations for rural deans.

---

1 Ecclesiastical Commissioners Act 1836.
2 Canon C23.
3 Church of England Miscellaneous Provisions Measure 2000, s12(4).

Appointment

The appointment of a rural dean is handled differently in each diocese. It is usually after consultation (or even election) by the clergy of a deanery, but is ultimately made by the bishop of the diocese.[4] The rural dean is commissioned rather than licensed. The bishop may appoint a temporary rural dean if the rural dean is ill,[5] and may appoint more than one person to fulfil the task jointly.[6] The rural dean is usually a member of the stipendiary clergy of the deanery, but there is no reason why this has to be the case. A self-supporting minister, or retired minister, could just as well be appointed, and may in some circumstances have more time to commit to the task.

The authority of the rural dean

In general the rural dean's role is one in which authority is derived from the bishop (in matters of pastoral care) or from the archdeacon (in matters relating to the care of churches and pastoral reorganization). Since, therefore, rural deans act on behalf of others, the ultimate responsibility for the duties which they exercise will always rest elsewhere.

Duties of the rural dean

The legal duties of the rural dean are set out below. However, it is clear that the role is one which can be fulfilled in a whole range of ways according to the gifts of the rural dean and the expectations of the diocese. Nonetheless, here are the bald facts.

1 Reporting to the bishop:
  • Pastoral situation of the clergy.
  • Vacancy in the deanery.

---

4 Church of England Miscellaneous Provisions Measure 2000, s12(1).
5 Church of England Miscellaneous Provisions Measure 2000, s12(1).
6 Church of England Miscellaneous Provisions Measure 2000, s12(2).

- Provision of services during a vacancy.
- Any ministers officiating without proper authority.
- Any matter it may be useful for the bishop to know.[7]

2 Investigating and reporting to the bishop the reasons for a parish:
- Not having an electoral roll.
- Not maintaining a PCC.
- Not holding an APCM.[8]

3 Reporting to the archdeacon:
- Defects in the fabric, ornaments or furniture of a church.
- That a building is in disrepair.[9]

4 The rural dean is a joint chairman (with a member of the House of Laity) of the deanery synod.[10]

5 The rural dean presides over the regular meetings of the chapter.

6 A rural dean may nominate a candidate to be a reader, after consultation with the minister of the candidate's parish, when that person's ministry is to be across the deanery.[11]

7 Together with the churchwardens, during a vacancy, the rural dean may apply to the bishop for a lay person to be authorized to distribute the Holy Communion.[12]

8 On behalf of the archdeacon, the rural dean should, if requested, inspect the terrier and inventory in the parishes of the deanery at least every three years.[13]

9 On behalf of the archdeacon, the rural dean should, if requested, survey the churches and churchyards of the deanery at least once every three years.[14]

---

7 Canon C23(1).
8 Canon C23(2).
9 Canon C23(3).
10 Canon C23(4) and Church Representation Rules, rule 28(1)(a).
11 Canon E5(1).
12 Canon B12(3) and Regulations on the Administration of Holy Communion in the Supplementary Material at the rear of the Canons.
13 Canon F17(2). As to Terrier and Inventory, see Chapter 3.
14 Canon F18.

10 On various other occasions the rural dean takes the place of a minister of the parish during a vacancy for certain acts.[15]

11 In some elections (notably those to diocesan synod) the rural dean may in some dioceses be asked to act as returning officer for the electorate of the deanery House of Laity.[16]

12 The rural dean (with the lay chairman and secretary of the deanery synod) has a duty to ensure that during the period of an election to General Synod no papers or other literature form part of an official circulation or are distributed at a synod meeting which are likely to prejudice the election.[17]

The civic connection

Rural deans can hold a key place in the relationship between the church and the civic authority, both with the elected members who they are likely to meet on formal occasions and with the chief executive and other chief officers of the district or borough. Every opportunity should be taken to meet with the officers in order that good relationships can be established. This can be built on when there are opportunities or when problems need to be resolved. Contact with council/district offices for the purpose of making relationships should be sought and then kept alive over the years.

The archdeacons often welcome the chance to develop these working relationships, particularly where there are problems and opportunities concerning development of new areas of housing, redevelopment of church buildings or on parsonage house sites. A rural dean is a helpful route into such a discussion for an archdeacon.

---

15 These are mainly obscure and relate to things which will probably have happened anyway: Canon B2(3) (to seek permission to continue to use a service which is no longer authorized); Canon B42(5)(b) (to seek permission to use a service in a foreign language); Canon B43(12)(2) (consultations regarding the sharing of worship with other denominations); Canon B44(9)(a) (consultation regarding the establishment of an LEP); Canons D1(4), E4(2A), and E7(5) (requesting the authority of the bishop for readers, deaconesses or lay workers, respectively, to take services).

16 Church Representation Rules, rule 32(2).

17 Church Representation Rules, rule 39(7).

Lay chairman[18]

The post of lay chairman came into being in 1969.[19] The lay chairman is a servant of the deanery as a whole, and is answerable to the laity who are the electorate. The lay chairman and rural dean share the chairing of deanery synod meetings in whatever way they agree. It is important for a rural dean and lay chairman to develop a good working relationship.

Role and expectations

Every rural dean will lead a very different deanery, each with its own unique strengths and challenges. Further, rural deans will already have significant responsibilities in their own parish or other employment. All these things impact on the role of the rural dean. It is important, therefore, that rural deans seek to equip themselves with the skills needed to understand their role and its opportunities and limitations.

FAQs

What else is a rural dean expected to do?

There may be various other expectations contained in the diocesan regulations for rural deans. Two examples are:

1 The rural dean is to take care to pass on to the clergy of the deanery such instructions as shall be sent by the bishops and archdeacon for distribution.
2 The bishop expects rural deans to be well acquainted with each of the parishes in the deanery and to assist the clergy in their ministry by advice and encouragement.[20]

---

18 The term has never been made gender friendly in the Church Representation Rules.
19 Church Representation Rules, rule 28(1)(a).
20 Diocese of Chelmsford Handbook for Rural Deans.

What about visitations?

Each year (in most dioceses, some less frequently) archdeacons undertake a visitation upon their archdeaconry.[21] This is a formal legal process and involves four key stages: Citation, Articles of Enquiry, Presentment and Visitation Service. The purpose of the visitation may be described as follows:

- to inspect church buildings and ornaments;
- to inquire into the ministry of the clergy and the parish;
- to check on the administration of the parish;
- to obtain information about the state of the diocese;
- to admit the churchwardens to office;
- to preach and teach.[22]

The Citation is the legal summons to the visitation. Churchwardens for the past year are cited to attend to make presentation (Presentment) of their answers to the questions which the archdeacon asks in the Articles of Enquiry. The churchwardens-elect are summoned to attend a service for their admission into office. Each diocese does this process slightly differently, but in many places the rural dean is asked to visit the parish and make the inspections listed above in preparation for the Visitation Service. Lay chairmen also sometimes share in this annual visiting process.[23]

What happens when ...

... there is a vacant parish in the deanery?

The rural dean may well have a significant role to play when a parish or benefice in the deanery is vacant. Much of the responsibility for the vacancy will fall on the churchwardens, but they will need and value assistance in their increased responsibilities. Readers and other staff may need support and supervision. There

---

21 Canons G5 and G6.

22 Chelmsford Diocesan Handbook for Rural Deans.

23 On these visits the inspections under Canons F17(2) and F18 (see above) are made.

may be others in the vacant parish in need of some specific support (for example those exploring vocations, ordinands or readers in training) and the rural dean may have a role in helping them.

Where there is a vacancy, the rural dean has a specific responsibility for the authorization of headstones in churchyards under the diocesan churchyards regulations.[24] Rural deans who are not used to dealing with these need to familiarize themselves carefully and to be aware of the pastoral implications of their decisions for the families involved and for the future incumbent of the parish.

The rural dean will also have an important part to play in preparing for the new ministry by assisting the churchwardens in practical ways of welcoming their new minister, and in preparation of the welcome service for the new minister.

Resources you should have at your fingertips

• Diocesan Regulations for Rural or Area Deans.

• Diocesan Churchyard Regulations.

Useful links

• Church House Deaneries Group: www.chdg.org.uk

• An example of a Rural Dean's Handbook with lots of information is at www.chelmsford.anglican.org/cme. This includes a useful check-list for rural deans which can be taken and adapted. There is also a handbook for lay chairman at the same site.

---

24 See Chapter 8.

14

Faculties

A possible scenario

Following the successful fund-raising campaign by the new 'Friends' organization, you are approached by their chairman. Their committee has generously agreed to give the sum of £20,000 to the PCC on condition that it is used, by Easter, to purchase a new set of frontals. Is this a problem?

What you need to know

General principles

The canons require that churches and chapels in every parish be kept in good order and, as needed, be repaired. This is so that the church is fit to be called the House of God.[1] Further, the churchyard must be fenced, and the fences maintained, and the churchyards be kept in good order. This should be in a manner befitting consecrated ground.[2]

Works to all Church of England buildings (whether listed or not) have been controlled for many centuries by the Consistory Courts of the church. The faculty system is a judicial system now governed by legislation.[3] All works, alterations and additions to parish churches, their churchyards and contents require faculty approval. This requirement applies to consecrated buildings and land and other churches licensed for public worship.

---

1 Canon F13(1).
2 Canon B13(2).
3 The Care of Churches and Ecclesiastical Jurisdiction Measure 1991; The Faculty Jurisdiction Rules 2000.

A faculty is a permissive right to undertake works to a church building or its contents. It is the duty of the minister and church-wardens to obtain a faculty before carrying out any work.[4] Works undertaken without a faculty are illegal.[5] Any person undertaking works without a faculty may be liable to prosecution and may have to pay for reinstatement and legal costs.[6] A PCC would also be in breach of trust and a minister may face disciplinary proceedings.

Quinquennial report

Every five years there must be a formal inspection of the fabric of the church by an approved architect, known as the quinquennial inspection.[7] The diocese will usually notify the PCC when this is due and send a list of approved inspectors. The fee for this inspection is paid by the diocese, but the PCC is responsible for reviewing the report and taking any necessary action in consequence of it. The quinquennial report, produced following the inspection, will set out the current state of the fabric of the building and make recommendations (usually prioritized by the architect) as to repairs that are necessary.

The Diocesan Advisory Committee (DAC)

Every diocese has a DAC. When anyone applies for a faculty the DAC is involved, so it is helpful to start by understanding its role. The functions of the DAC are, briefly:

- To act as an advisory body on matters affecting places of worship in the diocese and in particular to advise the bishop, chancellor, archdeacons, PCCs and any applicants for faculties on matters including architecture, archaeology and the history of

---

4 Canon F13(3).

5 The Care of Churches and Ecclesiastical Jurisdiction Measure 1991, s11(1).

6 See for example *Re Icklesham Churchyard*, October 2007, Chichester Consistory Court.

7 Inspection of Churches Measure 1955, s1.

the place of worship, the use, care and design of places of worship including redundancy, and the use and care of the church, its contents and its churchyard.

- To assess the risk of loss or damage to archaeological or historic remains from any proposals to petitions for faculties.
- To create a record of all proposals to alter, conserve and repair churches in the diocese.
- To approve the appointments of all quinquennial inspectors for the care and conservation of church buildings.[8]

Making plans

The PCC has responsibility for the care and maintenance of the church and churchyard,[9] and also for co-operating with the minister in the mission of the parish.[10] These two duties together often mean that the PCC decides it is time to make a repair or a change to the church. However, final control over the church, contents and land rests with the chancellor of the diocese, acting on behalf of the bishop.[11] Much of the frustration that surrounds the faculty system would be eased if we all changed our mind-set. The PCC is not so much deciding what it will do, as deciding what it will ask permission to do. It is no different for the person who lives in a thatched cottage or some such listed building. They know perfectly well that they can't do work on the building without getting the right permissions first. The same is true of a church.

Consulting in advance

As discussions develop as to what you want to do to the church or churchyard, you will need to bear in mind that at a later stage other people will have the right to know about it. So think this

---

8 The Care of Churches and Ecclesiastical Jurisdiction Measure 1991, Schedule 2.

9 Canon F13(1) and F13(2).

10 Parochial Church Councils (Powers) Measure 1956, s2(1).

11 The Care of Churches and Ecclesiastical Jurisdiction Measure 1991, s11(1).

through from the start. Always make sure that all the people who have a concern are consulted. This will of course be the PCC and perhaps also the congregation, but if the plans are for a major re-ordering or for something which could prove controversial it is wise to consult widely at an early stage. When formal faculty proceedings happen at a later time 'any person appearing to have a sufficient interest' may object,[12] so it is worth getting ahead of the game. You should also consult with your archdeacon and DAC at an early stage as they can often give good advice. Check on-line at your diocesan web-site to see if there is an advice leaflet available on the subject in question. Many DACs publish a wide range of advice which can save time later.

Depending on the type of work involved you may need a professional such as an architect or conservationist. The sooner they are part of your conversations the better. The time then comes when it is possible to draw up detailed plans and get specifications for the work.

Making the decision

Next, for most work on a church or a churchyard, the PCC will need to pass a resolution to do the work or make the change. This resolution is often in the form of an instruction 'that the minister and churchwardens apply for a faculty to do such and such a piece of work according to the specification supplied by X'. That way it is clear what is being agreed.

Statement of Need and Statement of Significance

If the building is listed you will need to prepare two documents ready for your faculty application, as well as the plans. A Statement of Need explains why you believe it is important to undertake this work – especially if it would have a serious impact on the layout or setting of the building. A Statement of Significance sets out the proposals in detail, and indicates the impact they would

---

12 The Care of Churches and Ecclesiastical Jurisdiction Measure 1991, s16.

have on the church as a building of architectural or historic importance. These documents can be prepared during the informal consultation process so that they are ready for the next stage.[13]

DAC consultation

The next step, even if you have already been in touch with the DAC, is to send the papers to that committee for a formal consultation to take place.[14] After the consultation, the secretary will issue a certificate indicating whether the DAC endorses your proposal, opposes it, or adopts a neutral stance. Quite often, the DAC will make some recommendation as to conditions that should be imposed by the chancellor or archdeacon (for example, in relation to archaeology). Matters such as this are likely to have been raised with you during the course of the consultation.[15]

Sometimes the consultation with the DAC will be a purely paper exercise, but quite often it involves a visit to your church by two or three members of the DAC, who then report their findings to the next meeting. You are likely to find that the DAC's insights will help you put your project into a wider context, and you may find that you will want to review your approach to the project in the light of their comments. This is why it is important to involve the DAC at an early stage and certainly before much money is spent.

The certificate is sent to you, and in many dioceses the petition for faculty and the public notice are also sent by the DAC secretary. In some dioceses they are to be downloaded from the Internet, but if you are unsure which form to use, check with the DAC secretary. The legal process can now begin.

Further consultation

The DAC will advise if you need to consult external bodies such as English Heritage, the local planning authority or any of the

---

13 Faculty Jurisdiction Rules 2000, rule 3(3).

14 The Care of Churches and Ecclesiastical Jurisdiction Measure 1991, s15.

15 Faculty Jurisdiction Rules 2000, rule 3.

amenity societies.[16] If so, you will need to send that body a complete set of papers, and invite their comments on your proposals. You may find that a further round of consultation with the DAC will then be necessary, if your own plans are modified in the light of comments received from one of them.[17]

The petition

Once the DAC has issued its certificate the formal proceedings can begin. These are couched in the vocabulary of court proceedings, because that is just what they are. Someone will need to petition the court and its judge, the chancellor, for permission to do the work. The petitioners are usually the minister and the churchwardens, although this does not have to be the case. The DAC or the diocesan registry will have sent you, or advised you, as to the correct forms to complete.

When you have completed the petition, you should send it to the registry together with the DAC certificate, a copy of the PCC resolution approving the work signed by the PCC secretary, a copy of the public notice (see below), and detailed plans, specifications, estimates or other descriptive material (as applicable). In some cases, further documents are needed.

If you are doing work which involves electrical installations or scaffolding, you will need to produce a simple letter of consent from your insurers, confirming that they are aware of the work you wish to do, and will continue to hold the building insured. If you have received a grant at any time in the past from English Heritage, or if the church is listed as grade I or grade II*, you will need to produce a letter from English Heritage confirming their agreement (in accordance with the conditions imposed at the time when you received the previous grant from them). If the work you are undertaking may require planning consent, you will need to produce the consent, or a letter from the local planning

---

16 These are the Ancient Monument Society (before 1715), the Council for British Archaeology, The Georgian Group (1700–1840), the Society for the Protection of Ancient Buildings (usually up to 1714), the Victorian Society (1847–1914) and the Twentieth Century Society (1914 onwards).

17 Faculty Jurisdiction Rules 2000, rule 3(3).

authority confirming that they do not consider that they should be involved.[18]

Fees

There is a fee payable for an application for a faculty. Practice varies from place to place, but in most dioceses, where a faculty petition is submitted by a parish, the diocese will pay the fee. If other people petition for a faculty, as they can (most often for a memorial in a churchyard), they have to pay the fee. Court fees and other legal costs may arise if the petition is opposed by objectors to the proposals. If the matter is likely to be contested, you will be made aware of this at an early stage. This is another reason to do your homework and consult everyone at an early stage. It is cheaper to meet objectors out of court than in!

The public notice

Anyone who lives in the parish has an interest in the parish church. It is for this reason that when you apply for a faculty you have to display a public notice informing people of what is planned and that they have a right to object if they wish. You will need to put up this public notice for 28 days in a prominent location.[19] The petition for faculty and the plans can be sent to the registry before the certified public notice, which can follow once the 28 days are over. However, a copy of the public notice in the form being displayed should be sent with the petition.

The decision

The chancellor (or possibly the archdeacon) then decides whether to grant the faculty. The chancellor may decide for or against the proposal whether or not anyone has objected. After a faculty has been granted, and the work has been implemented, it will be the duty of the petitioners to ensure that a copy of the completion

---

18 Faculty Jurisdiction Rules 2000, rule 4.
19 Faculty Jurisdiction Rules 2000, rule 6.

certificate is kept with the parish records, and further copies are sent to the registrar and the archdeacon.

Other situations

Most of the above has assumed that we are talking about repairs to the building or reordering inside a church but there are a few other matters worth mentioning. Generally anything that needs to be done inside or outside a church requires a faculty. This may include demolition of a church (including partial demolition), church extensions and the introduction or sale of church goods or ornaments, disinterment and reinterments, erection of a memorial in a churchyard and reservation of a grave-space.[20] In all such cases it is wise to consult the registry early, who will give instructions on the procedure to be followed.

De Minimis

In each diocese the chancellor will have produced a list of works which are considered minimal enough to not require a faculty. This is called the *De Minimis* list. Each chancellor's regulations are slightly different, but they usually permit minor repairs in the order of a couple of thousand pounds, sometimes with the consent of the archdeacon being required. There will usually also be a list of specific items and works which do not require a faculty. All other work does.

Headstone regulations

It is usual for the chancellor of the diocese to delegate limited authority over the churchyard to the minister of the parish. This will mean that it is not necessary to apply for a faculty every time a headstone is to be introduced. If the desired stone is within the terms of the delegated authority, which will set out some very specific parameters, then the incumbent may give permission and the family do not need to apply for a faculty. If they want some-

---

20 See Chapter 8.

thing that is not covered by the delegated authority they may still apply for a faculty, and ask the chancellor to give permission to put the stone into the churchyard. However, be warned that since the chancellor wrote the headstone regulations, a case will have to be made as to why that alternative stone should be allowed.

FAQs

Why do we need all this regulation?

Churches are historic buildings, which are part of the heritage of the land as well as places of worship. They are inherited by us and are to be passed on to others. It is necessary, therefore, to have some guidelines as to how they should be cared for and maintained. This protects the building from the temporary whim of any one generation, while ensuring that its use for the mission of the church can continue. The system also means that there is much free expert advice available to those who have responsibility, so think of the faculty system as a resource rather than a restriction.

Do I need a faculty?

I sometimes put it this way, somewhat controversially, when training clergy: 'Only a fool asks: do I need a faculty? The correct question is: is there any reason why I do not need a faculty?' Then the assumption is the right way round. You do not need a faculty if the proposal falls within your diocesan chancellor's *De Minimis* regulations. In all other cases, start out with the assumption that you do. Then, if the registry advises that there is no need, you can only be pleased.

Who may apply for a faculty?

The law sets out three groups who may apply: the archdeacon, the incumbent and churchwardens, or any other person appearing to have a sufficient interest. In parish matters it is usual for the incumbent and churchwardens to apply, but if two other PCC members signed the petition on behalf of the PCC they would appear to have sufficient interest.[21]

Can we appeal?

Yes. An appeal exists to the Court of Arches in the Canterbury province and the Chancery Court of York in the York province. An application for appeal must be made on a point of law and can only go ahead with the agreement of either the chancellor or the appeal court. The time limit is 28 days from judgement. The appeal court is presided over by either the Dean of Arches or the Auditor of the Chancery Court (in fact the same person) who sits with two diocesan chancellors from dioceses other than the source of the appeal. Together they determine the appeal.

I have heard of an archdeacon's certificate; what is that?

There was something called an archdeacon's certificate before 1991. Since then it no longer exists, although some faculties can now be granted by the archdeacon. It will be for the registry to decide which faculties this applies to, so there is no need for petitioners to worry about this.[22]

What is the ecclesiastical exemption?

Church buildings enjoy exemption from listed building consent and conservation area consent if certain conditions are met.[23] This is known as the ecclesiastical exemption. Since 1994 the exemption has applied only to those denominations that have created an 'approved system of control'. The Church of England's system of planning control, the faculty jurisdiction, has been recognized by the Secretary of State as an approved system of control and it

---

21 The Care of Churches and Ecclesiastical Jurisdiction Measure 1991, s16.

22 The Care of Churches and Ecclesiastical Jurisdiction Measure 1991, s14.

23 This exemption originates from the Ancient Monuments Consolidation and Amendment Act 1913.

has been agreed that the exemption from listed building control may continue, although there are many in the heritage movement who would like to end the exemption. Their evidence for asking this is that too many clergy and PCCs don't take faculty jurisdiction seriously. If the Church of England lost the exemption, then all work on listed buildings would still be subject to regulation. The local council's listed building officer and planning committee would become the people who decide what may or may not be done. These people may or may not have any interest in or care for the work and ministry of the church, whereas the DAC and the chancellor are experts and practising Christians who have a vast understanding of both the system of regulation and the purpose of the church. There can be no doubt that the church is best served by keeping the ecclesiastical exemption and working positively with faculty jurisdiction. Otherwise there is a danger that churches will be turned into museums in which worship is allowed.

Do I need planning permission as well?

Planning permission is required for any work to an existing building which changes its external appearance, or a material change of use of a building, or a new building, or an extension to a building. This will be in addition to faculty permission. Ask the registry if you are unsure.

Can we make some temporary changes to see how they work out?

There is power for the archdeacon to give a licence for temporary work to be done where no structural alterations are involved and where it would be possible to reinstate the work if necessary. The period of the licence cannot exceed 15 months. The request for such a licence requires the support of the minister and the majority of the PCC.[24]

---

24 Faculty Jurisdiction Rules 2000, rule 9.

What happens when ...

... *someone objects?*

Anyone with an interest, which includes parishioners and the local planning authority as well as the other consultees, may object to a faculty application. When this happens, the chancellor has to decide whether to grant the petition or not. This may be done by negotiating an agreement, or if necessary by a court hearing. When the public notice is displayed it explains how people may lodge an objection.

If there is a hearing, the chancellor will sit in a Consistory Court and will assess and analyse the evidence. The burden of proof lies with the petitioners. In the most difficult or controversial cases the court applies what are sometimes called the Bishopsgate Questions. These are:

- Have the petitioners proved a necessity for the proposed works?
- If yes, will the works adversely affect the character of a church as a building of special architectural and historic interest?
- If so, is the necessity such that in the exercise of the court's discretion a faculty should be granted?[25]

The chancellor will present his or her judgement verbally at the end of the hearing or at a later date in writing. Remember, the final decision belongs to the chancellor alone, so be wise enough to listen to advice from the various bodies along the way, but tenacious enough to not give up at the first hurdle.

... *we forget to apply for a faculty?*

Oh dear! The first rule is, don't bury your head in the sand. It won't help. In the worst case, the archdeacon may take you to court for failing to get a faculty. In practice the archdeacon and the registry will usually help you to apply for a retrospective confirmatory faculty which may legitimize unauthorized works. You

---

25 See *Re St Luke Maidstone* [1995] Fam 1 [1995] All ER 321.

may well have to pay the fees and any court costs. Expect to get your knuckles rapped, learn your lesson and do it right next time. You will survive!

... someone offers a gift to the church?

Generosity is not to be scoffed at, but gifts can sometimes cause a problem. If someone proposes to offer a gift to the church it may be wise to say from the outset that the parish can only accept it subject to faculty permission to introduce it to the church or churchyard. The best practice is always to enter into discussion with someone and explain the situation, and at all costs avoid getting cornered into accepting a gift before you have taken all the right steps to get permission.

... there is an emergency?

Everyone's definition of an emergency is different, but when the need is real the chancellor can usually give permission to go ahead quite quickly, if necessary by telephone. In such circumstances ring the registry or your archdeacon immediately you discover the problem. What will not be approved is something which has only become an emergency because you did not plan ahead. So for example, if the builders turn up, and you suddenly remember you forgot to get a faculty, that is not an emergency. If the wind causes damage to the church and you need to make it secure for people to enter or to pass by safely, that may be an emergency.

... we need to change things as building works progress?

When a faculty is granted it sets out what work may be done. If as you progress that needs to be changed in any substantial way, you will need to go back to the registry and the chancellor. Your professional advisers will help you to know when this is necessary if they are employed on a project. In any case where you are unsure whether the current faculty will cover a change you need to consult the registry.

Resources you should have at your fingertips

- In many dioceses the DAC has produced a range of advice leaflets to help parishes in their thinking about projects and ideas. Check out what is available in your diocese.

- *De Minimis* regulations for each diocese are usually contained in the diocesan handbook or may be on the diocesan web-site. You can always ask the registry for a copy.

- If you have never applied for a faculty before, ring the registry and ask for a set of papers, before you need them. Then you will have a better idea of what is involved. I am sure they will be only too pleased that you want to learn.

Useful links

- Many diocesan web-sites have lots of information on them from the DAC. Explore this and find out all you can. Try these sites too:
  www.english-heritage.org.uk
  www.churchcare.co.uk
  www.buildingconservation.com
  www.abetterview.co.uk
  www.historicchurches.org.uk
  www.fundsforhistoricbuildings.org.uk

- Your Diocesan Registry Clerk and DAC secretary are often a mine of information as they are handling these matters all the time. Most are very pleased to be asked to help. I have not yet met anyone in either role who was unwilling to help in every possible way.

15

Worship

A possible scenario

You are not looking forward to tonight's PCC. The vicar wants to change the services and you and a few friends plan to object. Unfortunately, you know that the vicar will get his own way – he always does and there is nothing you can do about it – or is there?

What you need to know

What services may be used

The forms of public worship in the Church of England are governed by statute and canon. The General Synod of the Church of England is permitted to authorize services in addition to the Book of Common Prayer, which remains the norm for all services if authorized alternatives are not used.[1]

Ministers must use only the forms of service authorized by canon,[2] although they have limited discretion to make minor changes within authorized services.[3] It is the minister's responsibility to have a good understanding of the forms of service used and to ensure that the worship offered glorifies God and enlightens the people.[4]

---

1 Church of England (Worship and Doctrine) Measure 1974.
2 Canon B1(2).
3 Canon B5.
4 Canon B1(2).

Authorized and commended services

General Synod may approve forms of services for use in the Church of England and amend any form of service so approved.[5] A current list of all the authorized alternative services is set out in the table below. The House of Bishops may also commend services. These are not authorized services, but by commending a service the House is indicating that, if a minister having the cure of souls wishes to use his or her discretion under Canon B5, then these services may be appropriate for use. These are also set out in the table.

A Authorized services

1 Calendar.
2 A Service of the Word.
3 Schedule of permitted variations to The Book of Common Prayer orders for Morning and Evening Prayer where these occur in *Common Worship*.
4 Prayers for Various Occasions.
5 The Litany.
6 Authorized Forms of Confession and Absolution.
7 Creeds and Authorized Affirmations of Faith.
8 The Lord's Prayer.
9 The Order for the Celebration of Holy Communion.
10 Collects and Post-Communions.
11 Rules for Regulating Authorized Forms of Service.
12 The Lectionary.
13 Opening Canticles at Morning and Evening Prayer; Gospel canticles; Other Canticles; A Song of Praise (Epiphany); Te Deum Laudamus.[6]
14 Holy Baptism.
15 The Eucharist with Baptism and Confirmation together with Affirmation of Baptismal Faith and Reception into the Communion of the Church of England (various tables authorize

---

5 Canon B2(1).

6 Services 1–13 are published in *Common Worship: Services and Prayers for the Church of England*.

the separate administration of Baptism, Confirmation, Affirmation of Baptismal Faith and Reception into the Communion of the Church of England in various contexts).[7]

16 Wholeness and Healing.

17 The Marriage Service with prayers and other resources.

18 Thanksgiving for the Gift of a Child.

19 The Funeral Service with prayers and other resources.

20 Series One Solemnization of Matrimony.

21 Series One Burial Services.[8]

22 Public Worship with Communion by Extension (NB explicit permission must be obtained from the bishop for the use of this rite).

23 *Common Worship* Ordination Service.[9]

24 Weekday Lectionary.[10]

25 A Service for Remembrance Sunday.[11]

26 Canticles 19, 22, 23, 25, 29, 34, 36, 40, 41, 46, 57, 58, 62, 65, 66, 72, 75, 77, 82 in *Common Worship: Daily Prayer*.

B Services which comply with the provisions of a Service of the Word[12]

1 An Order for Morning Prayer on Sunday.

2 An Order for Evening Prayer on Sunday.

3 An Order for Night Prayer (Compline).

4 An Order for Night Prayer (Compline) in Traditional Language.[13]

---

7 Services 14–15 published in *Common Worship: Initiation Services*.

8 Services 16–21 published in *Common Worship: Pastoral Services*.

9 Services 22–23 published separately.

10 Service 24 published in *Common Worship: Daily Prayer*. Services 1–24 are all authorized by General Synod for use until further notice.

11 Authorized by the archbishops under Canon B4(2) and published in *The Promise of His Glory*.

12 These are, therefore, authorized services.

13 Services 1–4 published in *Common Worship: Services and Prayers for the Church of England*.

5 During the Day.
6 Morning Prayer.
7 Evening Prayer.
8 Night Prayer.[14]
9 Sample services contained in *New Patterns for Worship.*

C Commended services and resources[15]

1 Introduction to Morning and Evening Prayer on Sunday.
2 Introduction to Holy Baptism.
3 Short Prefaces for the Sundays before Lent and after Trinity.
4 Additional Canticles.[16]
5 Additional Blessings.[17]
6 An Order for Prayer and Dedication after a Civil Marriage.
7 Thanksgiving for Marriage.
8 Ministry at the Time of Death.
9 Receiving the Coffin at Church before the Funeral.
10 Funeral of a Child: Outline Orders and Resources.
11 At Home after the Funeral.
12 Memorial Services: Outline Orders and Sample Service.
13 Prayers for Use with the Dying and a Funeral and Memorial Service.
14 Canticles for Marriages, Funerals and Memorial Services.[18]
15 Material contained in *New Patterns for Worship.*
16 *The Promise of His Glory*: Services and Prayers from All Saints to Candlemas.
17 *Lent, Holy Week, Easter*: Services and Prayers.
18 Other parts of *Common Worship: Daily Prayer* not mentioned above.

---

14 Services 5–8 published in *Common Worship: Daily Prayer.*

15 Material commended by the House of Bishops as being suitable for use by ministers in exercise of their discretion under Canon B5.

16 Services 1–4 published in *Common Worship: Services and Prayers for the Church of England.*

17 Service 5 published in the President's Edition of *Common Worship.*

18 Services 6–14 published in *Common Worship: Pastoral Services.*

D Versions of the Bible and of the Psalms

The following may be used in Book of Common Prayer Services
(with permission of the PCC) instead of the Authorized Version
of the Bible and the Psalter in the Book of Common Prayer.[19]

Bibles

1 Revised Version.
2 Revised Standard Version.
3 Good News Bible.
4 New English Bible.
5 Jerusalem Bible.

Psalters

1 The Revised Psalter.
2 The Liturgical Psalter (originally *The Psalms: A New Transla-
tion for Worship*, London, William Collins, 1977).

Any version of the Bible or Psalter may be used with Alternative
Services and Commended Services.

Services on Sundays and feast days

The canons set out what services will be used on Sundays. Morning and Evening Prayer must be said or sung in every parish church
at least on all Sundays and other principal feast days, and also
on Ash Wednesday and Good Friday.[20] Holy Communion must
be celebrated in every parish church on all Sundays and principal feast days, and on Ash Wednesday and Maundy Thursday.[21]
Holy Communion must be celebrated as regularly and frequently
as may be convenient.[22] The celebration of the Holy Communion

---

19 By virtue of the Prayer Book (Versions of the Bible) Measure 1965.
20 Canon B11(1).
21 Canon B14(1).
22 Canon B14(3).

in any parish church may only be dispensed with in accordance with the provisions of Canon B14A.[23]

Mid-week services

There are three canons which speak of Morning and Evening Prayer and at first sight they do not sit wholly comfortably together. It is the obligation of every bishop, priest, and deacon to say Morning and Evening Prayer daily, either privately or openly, subject to sickness or some other urgent cause.[24] This is clearly a personal obligation and is part of the canon which speaks of the lifestyle of the minister. It is also an obligation for a minister who has the cure of souls of a parish to see that Morning and Evening Prayer are said daily in the church, or one of the churches, in which they minister.[25] This would seem to suggest that while all clergy must say the office, those who have the cure of souls will usually say it in church, despite canon C26.1 allowing it to be said privately. The fact that the minister must 'see' that they are said could mean it would be in order to arrange for others to do it.

When the canons speak of this from the perspective of the provision of services (section B) rather than from the perspective of the minister (section C) the obligation looks slightly different. On Ash Wednesday, Good Friday and all other principal feast days Morning and Evening Prayer must be said in every parish church. On all other days the minister of the parish, together with other ministers licensed to serve in the parish, must make provision for Morning and Evening Prayer to be said in the parish church. After consultation with the PCC, the services may be said elsewhere if this serves to sustain the corporate spiritual life of the parish and the pattern of life of the ministers.[26] This encourages a corporate act (if there is more than one minister) and allows for the fact that these services are for the spiritual life of the parish, not just the minister's own rule of life. It also allows for the

---

23 Canon B14(2).
24 Canon C26(1).
25 Canon C24(1).
26 Canon B11(1) and 11.2.

service to be elsewhere than in the parish church. The minister may only say the offices elsewhere than in the parish church after consulting the PCC and if arrangements have been made for the services to be said in the parish church.

Looked at together it would certainly seem that best practice would be to say Morning and Evening Prayer in church, with others attending. In our modern world, where we often hear that the pattern of church attendance is changing so that people do not always come to worship on a Sunday, here is a real opportunity to develop mid-week congregations at times which serve the spiritual life of the parish. Public notice must be given in the parish, by tolling the bell or other appropriate means, of the time and place where the prayers are to be said or sung.[27] The modern equivalent of the bell is probably the Sunday news sheet or the parish web-site, but there is still something to be said for the bell being rung so that those who are nearby know that the church is being used.

Variations

The minister who is to conduct the service may use discretion to make and use variations which are not of substantial importance in any authorized form of service (including the Book of Common Prayer) according to particular circumstances.[28] Any variations in forms of service must be reverent and seemly and not be contrary to, or indicative of any departure from, the doctrine of the Church of England in any essential matter.[29] Any uncertainties about these matters should be referred to the bishop.[30]

The minister having the cure of souls may, on occasions for which no provision is made, use forms of service considered suitable for those occasions and may permit another minister to use the said forms of service. For example, if a parish were to host a civic service for the local council, it may be thought inappropriate to use Holy Communion or Morning Prayer, and the incumbent

---

27 Canon B11(2).
28 Canon B5.1.
29 Canon B5(3).
30 Canon B5(4).

may decide to use some other form of service. Notice that the minister having the cure of souls is the only person who may decide this.[31]

Vesture

The Church of England does not attach any particular doctrinal significance to the various types of vesture which are permitted, and the vesture worn by the minister is not to be understood as implying any doctrines other than those now contained in the formularies of the Church of England.[32] A minister may not change the form of vesture in use in a church unless he has ascertained, by consultation with the PCC, that such changes will be acceptable. If there is disagreement the matter must be referred to the bishop.[33]

At Holy Communion the presiding minister must wear either a surplice or alb with scarf or stole. When a stole is worn, other customary vestments may be added.[34] At Morning and Evening Prayer on Sundays the minister must normally wear a surplice or alb with scarf or stole.[35] At the occasional offices (that is, baptisms, weddings and funerals) the minister must wear a surplice or alb with scarf or stole.[36]

Music

It is the duty of the minister to ensure that only such words and music are chosen as are appropriate to the worship and to the congregation.[37] Where there is an organist, choirmaster or director of music the minister must pay due heed to his or her advice and assistance in the choosing and ordering of music, but at all times the final responsibility and decision in these matters rests with

---

31 Canon B5(2).
32 Canon B8(1).
33 Canon B8(2).
34 Canon B8(3).
35 Canon B8(4).
36 Canon B8(5).
37 Canon B20(3).

the minister.[38] The task of appointing or dismissing an organist, choirmaster or director of music belongs to the minister with the agreement of the PCC. The only exception is if the archdeacon, in the case of termination of an appointment, considers that the circumstances are such that the requirement as to the agreement of the PCC should be dispensed with.[39]

Copyright

It is often the case, especially since the introduction of *Common Worship*, that a parish will wish to prepare service booklets or leaflets for general use or for a specific occasion. There is a very useful leaflet setting out all the requirements for such materials called *A Brief Guide to Liturgical Copyright. Liturgical Texts for Local Use: Copyright Information.* This is available from the Church of England web-site. Copyright permission over music can be obtained via Christian Copyright Licensing (Europe) Ltd (see below).

FAQs

Who decides on the form of service?

Decisions as to which of the authorized forms of service (including the Book of Common Prayer) are to be used in any church in a parish (other than the services for occasional offices) must be taken jointly by the minister and the PCC.[40] Note that this is simple and absolute. Many clergy believe that they can decide, but that is not the case.

The answer is slightly different for occasional offices (other than confirmation, where the bishop decides). The decision as to which form of service is to be used is made by the minister who is to conduct the service, but if the people concerned object beforehand to the use of the service selected by the minister and

---

38 Canon B20(2).
39 Canon B20(1).
40 Canon B3(1).

they cannot agree, the matter must be referred to the bishop for his decision.[41]

Who may lead?

Communion may only be consecrated and administered by an ordained minister.[42] The bishop may authorize readers and other licensed lay persons to read the services of Morning and Evening Prayer.[43] In addition the minister (or in a vacancy the church-wardens) may invite a suitable lay person to say Morning and Evening Prayer (save for the Absolution).[44] This means that there is quite a wide discretion to allow lay people to lead.

Who may preach in church?

A sermon must be preached in every parish church at least once each Sunday, except for some reasonable cause approved by the bishop.[45] The sermon must be preached by a minister, deaconess, reader or lay worker duly authorized in accordance with canon law. At the invitation of the minister and with the permission of the bishop other people may preach.[46] The preacher must seek, with care and sincerity, to minister the word of truth, to the glory of God and for the instruction of the people.[47]

If a lay person preaches regularly then it would be best to arrange for him or her to be trained and licensed as a reader. Other visiting preachers are permitted. If they preach regularly (for example, area representatives of mission agencies) then it is likely that they will already have the bishop's permission to offici-ate or licence to preach. Other people who come to speak on an occasional basis can, of course, always be allowed to speak at the discretion of the minister. You can give them a slot in the service,

---

41 Canon B3(4).
42 Canon B12(1).
43 Canons D1, E6 and E7.
44 Canon B11.
45 Canon B18(1).
46 Canon B18(2).
47 Canon B18(3).

and so long as the canon requiring that one sermon be preached on a Sunday in a parish church is fulfilled, there is no reason why they cannot speak. It is not entirely easy to define what a sermon is, but generally speaking the purpose of the requirement that those who preach are to be authorized is intended to protect the doctrine of the church. A sermon may, therefore, be said to be any address which concerns the church's doctrine.

What about lay ministry?

It would be easy to conclude from what has been said so far that the canons are stuck in their own clerical generation and are nothing but a hindrance to current patterns of lay ministry in church life. Even a leading academic in church law, Norman Doe, ends his chapter on the ministry of the laity by saying, 'the law of the Church of England is lagging behind theological developments which recognize the centrality of the ministry of the laity'.[48] But let's not throw the baby out with the bathwater.

While the canons say very little about lay ministry, they do not, on the whole, prevent it. There is no reason why lay people cannot be involved in reading the Bible, leading intercessions, praying with and for others, leading worship and music, giving testimony, and in all sorts of other ways.[49] Those who are to be eucharistic ministers of the bread and wine must always be authorized by the bishop.[50] Many dioceses now also have schemes for the commissioning of lay ministers or ministry teams, which are not contrary to the canons, but are regulated by the bishop's directions in the diocese concerned.

The canons only really speak of who may lead at Holy Communion and Morning and Evening Prayer. If there is a Family Service or other service in addition to the statutory services there is no restriction on who may lead so long as they have the approval of the minister.

The canons state that everyone at a service should audibly

---

48 Doe, *The Legal Framework of the Church of England*, p. 250.

49 Some of these are covered by Canon B12(4).

50 Canon B12(3) and the directions in the Supplementary Material at the rear of the canons.

make the responses appointed and join in where appropriate. They should give proper attention to the service and due reverence to the name of the Lord Jesus.[51] The minister of the parish must ensure that all worship is glorifying to God and instructive to the people.[52] The churchwardens have a duty to keep good order during the service.[53] Within these parameters, who does what can be negotiated with a great deal of creativity.

When can Morning Prayer, Evening Prayer and Holy Communion be dispensed with?

One question which often arises is whether and when it is permissible to change or reduce the statutory services. The reading of Morning and Evening Prayer or the celebration of the Holy Communion may be dispensed with on an occasional basis by the minister and the PCC acting jointly. If it is desired to dispense with services on a more regular basis the minister and the PCC jointly may ask the bishop to authorize this. In a multi-parish benefice, for example, this may be a necessity. In my experience, bishops are perfectly aware of the realities of ministerial life in such situations and will support a well-thought-through proposal. The bishop has a duty to be satisfied that there is good reason for doing so and must have regard to the frequency of services of Morning and Evening Prayer or the celebration of the Holy Communion (as the case may be) in other parish churches or places of worship in the benefice and must ensure that no church ceases altogether to be used for public worship.[54] It is clear that, if the bishop so permits, almost any pattern of worship can be lawful.

What sort of bread and wine may be used at Holy Communion?

The canons state that the bread used at Holy Communion should be of the best and purest wheat flour and may be leavened or

---

51 Canon B9.
52 Canon 1(2).
53 Canon E1(4).
54 Canon B11(3) and Canon B14A.

unleavened. The wine should be alcoholic.[55] There are plenty of companies who supply special bread and wine for Holy Communion, but provided these two simple rules are followed there is no reason why everyday or local produce cannot be used. The same companies can supply special breads for those with wheat allergies, and in practical terms there would probably be no objection to this, provided that the usual bread for most people is wheat based.

What happens when ...

... the minister and PCC cannot agree which services to have?

If there is disagreement as to which forms of service are to be used in church, then, while the disagreement continues, the forms of service in the Book of Common Prayer must be used. The only exception to this is where one of the alternative authorized services (see table above, p. 141) was in regular use during at least two of the four years immediately preceding the date of the disagreement, when the PCC may resolve that those other forms of service shall be used.[56] Notice that the minister may not decide this, only the PCC.

In other words, neither the minister nor the PCC can force a change, but the PCC can ensure the status quo provided that the service which has been used (for two of the last four years) is an authorized service. The PCC could, for example, force a return to a service used until the new vicar came a year ago and changed it!

It is much more common for disagreements to be about smaller matters, rather than the form of service itself. The variations within the service are at the discretion of the minister taking the service.[57] A PCC may decide to have *Common Worship Order One*, but the minister decides which options to use within it. A

---

55 Canons B17(2) and B17(3).
56 Canon B3(2).
57 Canon B5.

wise minister will, of course, consult widely, not least as this is an opportunity to teach on the meaning of our worship and all its options. I was once accused of 'changing everything' because I prayed 'Our Father, who art in heaven ...' rather than 'which art in heaven'. Passions run high over such matters and it is better to use pastoral skills and to build relationships than to stand on the canonical rights.

... someone requests home communion?

There is a duty on a minister to take communion to those who are unable to come to church and who request it.[58] It is common for a licence given by a bishop to a eucharistic minister, authorizing them to administer Holy Communion in church, also to permit them to administer Holy Communion to the sick in their homes.

... there is a deanery (or some such) service?

On an occasional basis, it is in order for the minister and the PCC jointly to decide to dispense with Morning or Evening Prayer, so for such occasions a joint decision to cancel the service is fine.[59]

Resources you should have at your fingertips

- The Church of England web-site has a range of material to support the use of *Common Worship*. This includes on-line access to all the approved and commended texts, as well as other material: www.cofe.anglican.org/worship/liturgy/commonworship

- The Book of Common Prayer is also available on-line at www.cofe.anglican.org/worship/liturgy/bcp

- The Copyright document referred to above is available at www.cofe.anglican.org/worship/downloads/litcopy.rtf

---

58 Canon B37(2).
59 Canon B14A.

Useful links

- There is a myriad of material on the web from which to resource worship. Some organizations require affiliation but are well worth the money. See www.praxisworship.org.uk/ and www. rscm.com

- The liturgical commission has recently launched a new site which is useful: www.transformingworship.org.uk

- The liturgical resource Visual Liturgy also has a web-site: www.visualliturgylive.net

- For more information on copyright law as it applies to churches and places of worship, please contact Christian Copyright Licensing (Europe) Ltd at www.ccli.co.uk/main.cfm

16

Parish Finance

A possible scenario

The parish is the smallest in a united benefice. Mr Strong has been treasurer for many years. His report to the APCM is always greeted with great warmth and appreciation (and a few quiet smiles). Everyone knows that the figures don't quite add up on both sides of the accounts. Fortunately, Mr Strong is totally trustworthy and that's all that really matters, so the APCM just thanks him for his efforts and reappoints him. Is this a problem?

What you need to know

The PCC and the Charities Act

The accounting, auditing and reporting regime for all charities, including Church of England PCCs, is contained in the Charities Act 1993. The law makes it clear that charities are accountable to the public for the resources they control. There are detailed provisions as to how this Act is to be put into practice.[1] The regulations have been applied specifically to PCCs[2] and a full handbook is available to purchase or to download from the Church of England web-site.[3] Until now the PCC has been an 'exempted' charity which has meant that PCCs have not needed to register with the Charity Commission. This is soon to change.[4] Your diocesan office will no doubt inform you as the changes

---

1 Charities (Accounts and Reports) Regulations 2005.
2 Church Accounting Regulations 2006.
3 *The Charities Act 1993 and the PCC* (3rd edn).
4 Charities Act 2006.

come into force, but broadly speaking registration will start with larger churches[5] and be rolled out over the next few years.[6] You are advised not to go ahead with registration without consulting your diocesan finance department, as it is important to get the paperwork right.[7]

The role of the PCC in financial matters

The PCC has certain legal responsibilities for finance. Every member of the PCC is equally responsible for the church's finances. It is clear that not every PCC member will be able to understand the details of finances and accounting matters, and it is all the more important that those who can, should!

The legal responsibilities of the PCC for finances are:

- Power to frame an annual budget for the work of the church.[8]
- Responsibility for the financial affairs of the church including the collection and administration of all moneys raised for church purposes.[9]
- Responsibility for proper accounting.[10]
- Reporting to the APCM as to the finances of the PCC.[11]

The treasurer is an officer of the PCC,[12] and serves the PCC by providing financial leadership at a strategic level. The role involves ensuring that there are essential controls and procedures in place for the proper management of charitable funds, but the treasurer does not replace the PCC as the body responsible for the

---

5 Those with an income over £100,000 in any year. Note, if a parish has an income over that sum in any year after the new Act comes into force (perhaps because a building project takes place or a large legacy or grant is received) they will need to register.

6 Charities Act 2006.

7 The National Church Institutions are co-ordinating this process and PCCs will be guided as to how to complete registration documents.

8 Parochial Church Council (Powers) Measure 1956, s7(i).

9 Parochial Church Council (Powers) Measure 1956, s4(2)(a).

10 Charities Act 1993 (see *The Charities Act 1993 and the PCC*).

11 Church Representation Rules, rule 8.

12 Church Representation Rules, Appx II, para. 1(e).

finances of the parish. This is important for treasurer and PCC alike to remember.

The role of the treasurer

The role of the treasurer may be summed up as follows:

- Assisting the PCC in setting an annual budget.
- Ensuring received income is banked and recorded.
- Making payments on behalf of the PCC.
- Keeping proper books and records.
- Monitoring income and expenditure.
- Providing general financial information and reports to the PCC.
- Preparing the annual accounts and financial report.

The treasurer must ensure that appropriate financial checks and balances are in place, but the PCC is responsible for the proper use of church funds. Anyone who takes on the role of treasurer for a PCC desires and deserves proper training and support. Most dioceses offer such support. If there is a fee for this training the PCC should be prepared to pay it.

In many parishes, and especially in larger parishes, the role can be large and complex. There is usually only one PCC treasurer,[13] but that does not mean he or she must do everything. It is perfectly possible for the treasurer to have some help. There may be assistant treasurers (a good way of doing some succession planning), or a bookkeeper, a cashier, and a gift-aid secretary. Each of these roles can assist the treasurer and make the work a shared and manageable task. If a number of people are involved it is vital that each has a written description of the task they are being asked to do. It would be wise, for everyone's protection, if all such appointments are made by the PCC rather than the incumbent or the treasurer.

---

13 Church Representation Rules, Appx II, para. 1(e)(i) allows for more than one person to be appointed jointly as treasurer.

Incumbents and finance

Many ministers are heard to say: 'I don't need to know about finance because I have a good treasurer.' While the latter may be true, the former is most certainly not! The PCC is a legal body,[14] and a charitable body, subject to regulation regarding its financial practice. As chairman of the PCC the minister has a responsibility to ensure that good financial practice is being followed. Clearly it is not good enough for the chairman to leave this function to the treasurer alone.

A minister needs a broad understanding of the annual accounts and usually oversees the production of the annual report. Finance is not just about paying bills and accounting. Part of a minister's responsibility is to teach about stewardship through both word and example. Not all clergy find this easy, but it is a very important part of ministry.

What needs to be in the annual report

The details of this are set out clearly in *The Charities Act and the PCC* (3rd edition) and there are full example documents to help. The report relates to the financial year ending the previous December. It must contain:

- A general statement of purpose for the parish.
- A list of names of members of the PCC and dates of service. Remember that this will often mean three groups of names: those who served from January until the APCM in the previous year, those serving from the APCM until December and those who served for the whole year.
- A description of how the parish is structured (committees etc.) and the names of members of committees.
- A report on the business of the PCC in the last year.
- A written statement of the financial affairs of the parish.

---

14 Parochial Church Council (Powers) Measure 1956 and Church Representation Rules.

- The parish accounts, examined or audited and agreed by the PCC.

The APCM will also have to receive a range of other reports[15] and it makes sense to combine them all in one document. Then you have one coherent 'Annual Report' which can be read by anyone. It should end up looking much like those of any other charity. This may sound complicated but the guidance and examples in *The Charities Act and the PCC* are very clear, making it perfectly possible to get it right. More than that, some of the items will change little from year to year, so once you have cracked the format it is not so hard the following year.

FAQs

Who appoints the treasurer and when?

The treasurer is appointed by the PCC[16] (not the APCM). The appointment should be made at the first meeting after the APCM. The treasurer can be a member of the PCC, or if no one is able to do it, may be appointed from outside their number.

What should a treasurer report to the PCC?

The treasurer should present a report on the state of the finances at each PCC meeting. My own practice is that this should be relatively high up the agenda and taken before any 'spending' items, so that the PCC knows whether they have any money to spend! A report to the PCC needs to be simple enough to understand and detailed enough to be meaningful. That usually means a report of income and expenditure to date, reference to the budget so that the figures have a context, and a report on the state of the 'funds' held by the parish, so that the overall position can be seen.

---

15 See chapter 4.
16 Church Representation Rules, Appx II, para. 1(e).

What are restricted, designated and unrestricted funds?

The words 'accounts' and 'funds' can be confusing. A PCC has one or more bank accounts. It is rare for the treasurer to need to tell the PCC what is in these accounts as they are, so to speak, in the background. The figures from those bank accounts (and elsewhere) are what form the parish accounts. So it is usually the parish accounts, not the bank accounts, the treasurer is talking about when he or she uses the word 'accounts'.

The actual cash held by the PCC is kept in 'funds' which may or may not correlate to bank accounts. Again, that's why the bank accounts are kept in the background! This is not the same as when we just talk about raising funds. It is a technical term. Funds are the way in which the money is divided into 'pots' for accounting purposes. These funds come in four types, unrestricted, designated, restricted, and endowment funds, and you need to know what these types mean. The guidance in *The Charities Act and the PCC* is detailed, but it seems to me that the best way to get a grip on this is to consider how the money came to the PCC and what the PCC can do with it.

Fund Type	How it got there	What you can do with it
Unrestricted	Any giving where the donor did not specify what it can be used for. This may be called the general fund, but other funds can meet this description.	The PCC can use it for any purpose it deems appropriate.
Designated	Any giving where the donor did not specify what it can be used for. The PCC can decide to set it aside for a designated purpose.	For the time being this money can only be used for the designated purpose, although the PCC has power to change its mind.

Restricted	Any giving where the donor gave for a specific purpose. 'This is for the fabric find, vicar!' or 'We're having a coffee morning to raise money for the new hymn books'.	This money can only be used for the purpose for which it has been given unless you go back to the donor and ask.
Endowment	Any giving which specified that you should invest the money and spend the proceeds of the investment.	The PCC can only spend the interest, not the capital.

As if life were not complicated enough, you may already have realized that more than one of these names can attach to a single fund, and that a single fund can have more than one type of money in it. Guidance for treasurers will set out in detail how to work this out, but for most people it is enough to understand the meaning of the different types of fund. Then at least when the treasurer announces at a PCC meeting that 'the Fabric Fund currently contains restricted and designated money, together with the unrestricted proceeds of an endowment fund' you can nod sagely as if he had spoken English! You should also know that the treasurer must account for the funds in this way, so it's no good shooting him.

When do we need an auditor?

The accounts of a parish need to be either audited or examined by an independent person. The APCM must appoint someone, failing which the PCC may do so.[17] The rules as to how accounts are prepared and an inspection is conducted vary according to the size of the income of the parish. The key figures are £100,000,

---

17 Church Representation Rules, rule 9(5)(d) and Church Representation Rules, Appx II, para 1(g).

£250,000 and £500,000. These rules are quite complex and if in doubt it would be wise to consult your diocesan accounts department. The table below sets out how the thresholds work.

Income threshold[18]	Accounts basis	Examination	Notes
Up to £100,000	Receipts and payments	Examination required	
£100,000– £250,000 Assets below £2.8m	Accruals	Examination required	
£250,000– £500,000 Assets below £2.8m	Accruals	Examination required	Examiner must be qualified under the Act[19]
£100,000– £500,000 Assets above £2.8m[20]	Accruals	Audit required	Examiner must be qualified under the Act
Over £500,000	Accruals	Audit required	Examiner must be qualified under the Act

Calculating these figures and thresholds involves taking the total of all income in all parts of the accounts and the book value of any assets owned by the PCC.[21]

---

18 These thresholds relate to income only.

19 This usually means a fully qualified accountant.

20 This would be where a parish owns property and other assets over this figure (for example the book value of the church hall and curate's house). It will not often happen, but could do so in some parishes.

21 For detailed guidance as to how these work out in practice see *The Charities Act and the PCC* (3rd edn) and Charities Act 2006. The table assumes that the new figures in the Charities Act 2006 are in force.

What moneys should be in the PCC accounts?

It is often true that all sorts of groups and activities in the church try to squirrel away their funds. The general rule is that money which is raised or spent on any activity for which the PCC is responsible or over which the PCC has control should be in the annual accounts as both income and expenditure. It is perfectly possible for a group (say, Young Wives) to run the account all year, but it must be added into the parish accounts and annual report at the end of the year. Once again, detailed guidance is in *The Charities Act and the PCC*, but in my experience the rule of thumb is: it probably should be in the PCC accounts unless there is a good reason why not! Start from that assumption and you won't go far wrong. There are often local trusts in parishes, frequently with the vicar and churchwarden as trustees. This money is not under the control of the PCC and is not, therefore, included in PCC accounts.

What expenses can the clergy claim?

A booklet is available about clergy expenses: *The Parochial Expenses of the Clergy. A Guide to their Reimbursement.* It can be downloaded from the Church of England web-site. A claim for the actual amount spent, backed by receipts, should be submitted monthly. It is important that there is agreement about what is being claimed, especially if it is above the usually agreed items stated in the booklet. Lump-sum payments should not normally be made as these can have tax implications for both the minister and the PCC. The PCC can only pay expenses that are claimed, but most ministers in fact claim less than the guidelines suggest, so PCCs need to have an informed and generous mind when it comes to these proper payments.

Are there any simple rules to follow for the handling of money?

- Two people should count the collections (cash and envelopes) as soon as possible, e.g. after the Sunday services. The people should not be related to each other, not be the same two each week and not always include the treasurer. The income details should be recorded in the service register and initialled by the counters.

- The amount in each envelope (planned-giving weekly envelopes or Gift Aid envelopes) should be recorded on the envelope or on a separate sheet and noted in the service register. The envelopes (and record sheet if used) should be passed to the Planned Giving Recorder.

- Money should be banked as soon as possible and left in the safe until it is banked. If it is necessary to take money home prior to banking, ensure that it is covered by your insurance.

- Cheque payments – all bank accounts should require two signatures on cheques and other instructions. Cheques should never be signed blank, therefore it is practical to have at least four signatories. A PCC resolution is necessary if you need to change bank signatories. There is no requirement for the incumbent or any other member of the clergy to be a signatory, although they may be. The list of signatories should be reviewed regularly, for example after each APCM.

- Payments should only be made against invoices or (in the case of expenses) receipts. If possible always make payments by cheque rather than cash.

- Expenses should be paid for actual expenses incurred and not be a set amount each month either to the vicar or to anyone else. Lump-sum payments may incur tax liabilities.

- Receipts should always be given for any cash received, for example a hall let. If possible, people should be encouraged always to pay by cheque, for example statutory fees from funeral directors.[22]

What about discretionary funds?

In some parishes the incumbent may be allowed a discretionary fund by the PCC. The nature of this fund is that most people will not know what the money is spent on, since the idea is to allow

---

22 Adapted from www.parishresources.org.uk.

the minister to have full discretion over it. The fund itself will not usually be part of the PCC accounts. If the source of the income is from the PCC, that will be recorded in the annual accounts.

Are the accounts a public document?

The annual report and accounts of a parish must be published, usually by displaying them on the noticeboard.[23] Periodic reports to the PCC will be recorded by the PCC secretary in the minutes, and there is usually no reason why this should not be seen by others. If there is nothing to hide, why not keep people as well informed as you can?

Can the PCC give away a tenth of its income?

Income is to be used for the charitable purposes of the PCC and it is quite in order for a PCC to decide that other charitable organizations (such as mission agencies) can benefit from unrestricted PCC funds. It is also appropriate for the church to be doing corporately what it wants individuals to be doing – tithing. Sometimes money is raised by the parish for another charity and in that case the money is a restricted fund. So money going to a charity, Christian Aid for example, may include restricted and unrestricted funds.[24]

What about Gift Aid?

The PCC should do all it can to encourage people to maximize their giving. The Gift Aid scheme is simple to administer and requires little of the giver other than a willing signature. There is a lot of advice available on Gift Aid, especially in the stewardship web-sites mentioned at the end of this chapter.

---

23 Church Representation Rules 9(3).
24 See *Legal Opinions concerning the Church of England*, p. 134.

What happens when ...

... *we can't find a treasurer?*

If the PCC cannot appoint a treasurer from its own number then it may appoint someone who is not a member of the PCC. That person does not automatically then become a PCC member, although they may well attend PCC meetings to report to the PCC and they could be co-opted. If no treasurer is appointed the task must be done by the churchwardens.[25]

... *a minister receives fees?*

Statutory fees, that is the legal fees set by General Synod, are charged for certain services, for example for weddings and funerals. The charges change from year to year and an updated list of fees should be displayed in church. The current table of fees is available from the Archbishops' Council. The fees a minister receives usually include sums for the PCC as well as money due to the minister, so it is important to devise a system for dealing with them accurately and regularly. All the clergy fees received in a parish technically belong to the incumbent, so where there are assistant clergy they should pass the fees to the incumbent who will deal with them appropriately.

Fees form part of the minister's stipend. They will affect the amount of stipend which is due from the diocese. Clergy must declare them annually to the diocese and also to HM Customs and Revenue. If a minister retains the fees received they will be deducted from the stipend due in the following year. To make it easier for clergy households it is possible for a minister to assign fees, that is to legally agree to send them to the diocese. This will involve paying them to the diocese once a month, and then the stipend a minister actually receives will be unaffected. Most clergy assign their fees. Some clergy leave the administration of assigned fees to their treasurers, but responsibility for what happens to the money remains with the minister.

In some parishes it is the practice for the minister to receive the

---

25 Church Representation Rules, Appx II, para. 1(e).

Easter offering. If this happens, the sum received will need to be declared and will be taken into account when stipend payments are made.

... a visiting minister takes a service for us?

In this case some ministers are entitled to a fee and others are not. Self-supporting ministers and readers have agreed that they will not charge for their ministry and they do not receive fees for Sunday services. If they receive fees for weddings and funerals they should usually (unless otherwise agreed by the minister) be passed to the minister of the parish. Retired ministers are in a different position. They are usually entitled to charge a fee for Sunday services. For occasional offices, there may well be diocesan directions as to what proportion of the fee the retired minister may keep. If a parish is in vacancy then the churchwardens are responsible for accounting for fee income and expenditure to the diocesan office, which will provide guidance.

... we are a group ministry or a team ministry?

Following the above principles, the basic accounting unit is a PCC. So in a team ministry, where there is usually only one PCC, the accounts of all the churches must be drawn together into one set of accounts for the Annual Meeting. In a group ministry, where there are several PCCs, each PCC must produce its own annual report and accounts. Likewise in a multi-parish benefice, each PCC must have its own accounts.

Resources you should have at your fingertips

The full details of what is required for accounting and reporting are set out in *The Charities Act and the PCC* (3rd edition) which can be downloaded from the Church of England web-site: www. cofe.anglican.org/info/finance/charitiesact.pdf. This book is vital for all treasurers and ministers. There is a version that relates only to smaller parishes, but generally, anyone who can cope should use the above version, so that you understand as much as you can.

Another useful source of information for a church treasurer is Robert Leach, *The Church Treasurer's Handbook*, Canterbury Press, Norwich, 2005.

Useful links

There are a number of useful websites in this area:

- Association of Church Treasurers: www.acat.uk.com/acat/index.htm

- The Church of England National Stewardship Adviser has put together a site at www.parishresources.org.uk which contains a vast amount of helpful material.

- Other sites which include good material are:
  Chichester Diocese www.stewardship.diochi.org.uk
  Liverpool Diocese: www.givingingrace.org
  Try your own diocesan web-site too!

- If you need more assistance, most diocesan finance departments have someone who can help. Ring your diocesan office and ask.

- The Church of England web-site also has a lot of resources: www.cofe.anglican.org/info/finance

- The booklet about clergy expenses mentioned above can be downloaded from www.cofe.anglican.org/lifeevents/ministry/workofmindiv/dracsc/parochialexpenses

- Information about clergy pay is available at www.cofe.anglican.org/info/clergypay

- A copy of each year's legal fee sheet is available from www.cofe.anglican.org/lifeevents/ministry/workofmindiv/dracsc

17

Ecumenism

A possible scenario

The local ministers' group gets on really well together. They discuss holding a joint service every month when they could take turns to lead, preach and preside at Holy Communion. There is also discussion as to whether you and the Methodists could actually share one building at some time in the future. What do you need to bear in mind?

What you need to know

The Ecumenical Relations Measure 1988

When a church is 'in communion' with the Church of England, ministry and orders are fully accepted by both sides. This is not so with other churches. However, the Church of England has set up procedures to enable it to share worship, ministry and mission with churches with whom it is not in communion.[1] As a result of this measure, two canons have been passed to facilitate ecumenical ministry.[2]

Leading shared worship

Canon B43 sets out the way in which invitations can be made to other Christians to lead worship in Church of England churches, and ministers of the Church of England can lead worship in

---

1 Church of England (Ecumenical Relations) Measure 1988.
2 Canons B43 and B44.

churches of other traditions. It provides the ground rules for those occasions when Church of England churches share in worship in the context of local 'Churches Together' or when they have signed a declaration of ecumenical welcome and commitment or at any other time.

Church of England ministers may invite ministers and lay people of other churches on an occasional basis to take part in the worship of the Church of England in a number of ways. Those who are invited must be baptized[3] and in good standing with their own churches. They must also be authorized to do similar duties in their own church. They may be invited, with the approval of the PCC, to:

- Say or sing Morning or Evening Prayer or the Litany.
- Read Holy Scripture at any service.
- Preach at any service.
- Lead intercessions at Holy Communion.
- Lead prayers at any other service.
- Assist at baptisms and weddings.[4]
- Conduct a funeral service.
- Assist in distributing the sacrament (bread or wine) at Holy Communion.[5]

In addition, the bishop's permission must be sought when regular invitations are proposed, and when someone is invited to preside at Holy Communion or take part in an ordination.[6]

Church of England clergy, lay workers and readers may accept invitations from other churches to share in their worship, provided that it only involves the kind of duties they perform in a Church of England church. Before accepting any invitation they will need the approval of the incumbent of the parish where the service is to take place and the approval of both the bishop and

---

3 Special arrangements exist for Quakers and Salvationists in this regard. The House of Bishops Guidelines of 1991 cover this. The bishop must be satisfied that special circumstances exist.

4 See Chapter 7 on involvement of other ministers at Church of England marriage ceremonies.

5 Canon B43(1).

6 Canon B43(2).

the PCC in that parish if the invitation is to take part in leading worship on a regular basis.[7] The bishop will need to be sure there are special circumstances before allowing a priest to accept an invitation to preside at Holy Communion in another church.[8]

Incumbents may also invite other churches to use Church of England churches for services in their own tradition, either on special occasions or more regularly. The invitation needs the approval of the PCC and the bishop – and the bishop will indicate any special conditions for the arrangement.[9] If a regular arrangement seems likely to become permanent, an agreement under the Sharing of Church Buildings Act may be appropriate.

As local churches of different traditions grow together, developing a common life and witness, it may be appropriate to work towards establishing a Local Ecumenical Partnership (LEP).

Partnership with other churches

The Church of England is able to participate in a Local Ecumenical Partnership, and Canon B44 sets out how a bishop can make an agreement with other Christian churches to put these arrangements in place. The bishop may make such an agreement with other designated churches.[10]

There are six types of LEP, known in ecumenical networks as Categories 1–6:

1 Single-congregation Partnerships – where two or more churches agree to establish a single congregation, usually in a shared building, which continues to take part actively in the life of each of its parent denominations.
2 Covenanted Partnerships – where two or more congregations from different traditions develop shared ministry and mission (and much else) while continuing to worship in their own churches.

---

7 Canons B43(3) and B43(6).
8 Canon B43(4).
9 Canon B43(9).
10 That is designated under Church of England (Ecumenical Relations Measure) 1988, see the list at the end of the chapter.

3 Shared Building Agreements – where two or more congregations from different traditions share the same building but continue to worship separately.
4 Chaplaincy Partnerships – where the churches appoint chaplains jointly to work in industry, colleges or in other non-congregational ministries.
5 Mission Partnerships – where the churches support joint mission projects in specific areas, often involving the local churches.
6 Education Partnerships – where the churches develop joint educational and training programmes.[11]

Any individual partnership may appear in more than one of these categories. For example, many single-congregation partnerships will operate in the context of a Shared Building Agreement.

Parish-based LEPs (Categories 1–3)

For a parish to become involved in an LEP, whether single congregation or a multi-congregational covenant:

• The incumbent must agree.
• The PCC must agree by at least a 75% majority.
• The parish's APCM (or a special meeting) must agree.
• The Diocesan Pastoral Committee must agree, after consultation with the Deanery Synod and Standing Committee.[12]

The Constitution of the LEP will need to include clauses that the LEP will be subject to review and renewal after not more than seven years. Any extension or amendment to the LEP must also have the consent of:

• The incumbents concerned.
• The PCCs concerned.
• The Diocesan Pastoral Committee.[13]

---

11 These are usually ascribed to Churches Together in England (CTE) documents from around 1994.
12 Canon B44(1).
13 Canon B44(2).

Extra-parochial LEPs (Categories 4–6)

When considering a Category 4, 5 or 6 LEP the bishop must make such consultations as he sees fit. The arrangements for any partnership in these circumstances simply need the approval of the Diocesan Pastoral Committee.[14]

Ecumenical officers

If issues arise regarding ecumenical relations it is always wise to seek out help. Each diocese will usually have a diocesan ecumenical officer, whose details will be available in the diocesan directory. Counties and equivalent areas also have officers who work on behalf of all the denominations in the area (for example Churches Together in Oxfordshire), and such a person is often known as the County Ecumenical Officer.[15]

FAQs

Can a Churches Together group make a contract of employment?

Generally the answer is no. A contract requires a legal body to enter into it, either an individual or a legal corporate body. For the Church of England that could be a PCC but for an informal grouping there is no such legal entity. This is probably why such groups usually establish a trust or work in the name of one of the denominations if they are making such an appointment.

What churches do Canons B43 and B44 apply to?

The following churches have been designated by the Archbishops of Canterbury and York as churches to which the 1988 Measure applies.

---

14 Canon B44(7).

15 For the local officer go to www.churches-together.net and click on 'networking'.

The Baptist Union
The Methodist Church
The Moravian Church
The Roman Catholic Church in England and Wales
The United Reformed Church
The Congregational Federation
The International Ministerial Council of Great Britain
    (formerly the Shiloh United Church of Christ)
The Lutheran Council of Great Britain
The Archdiocese of Thyatira and Great Britain
The Council of African and Afro-Caribbean Churches
The Free Church of England
The Southam Road Evangelical Church, Banbury
Member Churches of the Evangelical Church in Germany
Assemblies of God in Great Britain and Ireland
The New Testament Church of God
The Russian Patriarchal Church of Great Britain being
    the Orthodox Diocese of Sourozh operating within the
    provinces of Canterbury and York
The Independent Methodist Churches
The Church of the Augsburg Confession of Alsace and
    Lorraine
The Evangelical-Lutheran Church of France
The Reformed Church of Alsace and Lorraine
The Reformed Church of France[16]

What Churches are in communion with the Church of England?

The term 'in Communion with the Church of England' may be taken to include the following churches:

1 All member churches and extra-provincial dioceses of the Anglican Communion, including united churches which incorporate former Anglican churches.

---

16 See Supplementary Material at the back of *The Canons of the Church of England.*

Member churches

Anglican Church in Aotearoa, New Zealand and Polynesia
Anglican Church of Australia
Episcopal Anglican Church of Brazil
Episcopal Church of Burundi
Anglican Church of Canada
Church of the province of Central Africa
Anglican Church of the Central America Region
Anglican Church of the Congo
Hong Kong Sheng Kung Hui
Church of the province of the Indian Ocean
Church of Ireland
Anglican Communion in Japan
Episcopal Church in Jerusalem and the Middle East
Anglican Church of Kenya
Anglican Church of Korea
Church of the province of Melanesia
Anglican Church of Mexico
Church of the province of Myanmar (Burma)
Church of Nigeria (Anglican Communion)
Anglican Church of Papua New Guinea
Episcopal Church in the Philippines
Episcopal Church of Rwanda
Scottish Episcopal Church
Church of the province of South East Asia
Church of the province of Southern Africa
Anglican Church of the Southern Cone of America
Episcopal Church of the Sudan
Anglican Church of Tanzania
Church of the province of Uganda
Episcopal Church in the United States of America
Church in Wales
Church of the province of West Africa
Church in the province of the West Indies

Extra-provincial dioceses

Anglican Church of Bermuda
Anglican Church in Ceylon (Sri Lanka)
Episcopal Church of Cuba

Lusitanian Church of Portugal
Reformed Episcopal Church of Spain
Falkland Islands Jurisdiction
The Anglican Church in Venezuela
Episcopal Church of Puerto Rico

United churches incorporating former Anglican dioceses
Church of Bangladesh
Church of North India
Church of South India
Church of Pakistan

2 The Old Catholic churches of the Union of Utrecht.

Old Catholic Church in the Netherlands
Catholic Diocese of the Old Catholics in Germany
Christian Catholic Church of Switzerland
Old Catholic Church of Austria
Old Catholic Church of the Czech Republic
Polish National Catholic Church (USA)
Polish Catholic Church (Poland)
Old Catholic Church of Croatia

3 Philippine Independent Church.

4 Mar Thoma Syrian Church of Malabar.

5 Nordic and Baltic Lutheran churches which have approved the Porvoo Declaration. To date, these are:

Evangelical-Lutheran Church of Finland
Evangelical-Lutheran Church of Iceland
Church of Norway
Church of Sweden
Estonian Evangelical-Lutheran Church
Evangelical-Lutheran Church of Lithuania[17]

---

17 See Supplementary Material at the back of *The Canons of the Church of England*.

What is the Anglican–Methodist Covenant?

The signing of the Anglican–Methodist Covenant in 2003 brought about a special relationship between the Church of England and the Methodist Church. It did not change the provisions of the law but encouraged both denominations to work together in mission, ministry and worship where possible. Some bishops have put in place special arrangements to ease the process of inviting and responding to invitations under Canon B43 in the case of relations between the Church of England and the Methodist Church. Further details, documents and supporting texts are available on the Internet.[18]

What is a Bishop's Mission Order?

There is provision in the proposed Dioceses Pastoral and Mission Measure, which is not yet in force, for Mission Orders to be made to enable fresh expressions of church. These could include working with other denominations.[19]

What happens when ...

... the Anglican church is the only church in the neighbourhood?

After consultation with other churches in the wider area, parish churches where there are no immediately neighbouring churches from other traditions are encouraged to acknowledge publicly their hospitality to Christians from other churches through making a Declaration of Ecumenical Welcome and Commitment. Information about such a commitment can be received from the Ecumenical Officer in your diocese.[20]

---

18 At www.anglican-methodist.org.uk where there are also other useful documents and guidelines for ecumenical work (click on 'Resources for Diocesan and District Ecumenical Officers').

19 Note that the new legislation is not yet in force.

20 A resource sheet is available from www.anglican-methodist.org.uk/ddeo_catA.htm.

... *we want to work with a church not on the designated list?*

It is only possible to enter into an LEP with churches on the designated list. However, a Shared Building Agreement does not have to be attached to an LEP, so it may be possible to work in some ways with such a denomination.[21] Shared Building Agreements can be made with any of the churches designated under that Act. The lists are not the same.[22] Churches not designated under the Ecumenical Relations Measure 1988 may hold their own services on the basis of the Sharing Agreement (which relates solely to the building). Shared worship, however, will be regulated by Canon B43 and would not be possible with a church not designated under the 1988 Measure.

Resources you should have at your fingertips

Canons B43 and B44.

Useful links

- There is lots of information about ecumenical matters at the website of Churches Together in England, www.churches-together. net

- A comprehensive range of guidance notes is also available for ecumenical officers in the CCU Resources pack which can be downloaded from www.anglican-methodist.org.uk

---

21 Sharing of Church Buildings Act 1969.

22 The list for this purpose is available at www.anglican-methodist. org.uk/ddeo_catB.htm: Sharing of Church Buildings Act 1969, Sch 2.

18

Employing Staff

A possible scenario

The PCC decides to employ a youth worker. They want to make the money go as far as possible and keep things simple. What do they need to know?

What you need to know

Generally

More and more churches now employ staff in one form or another. It is vital to remember that this means you are taking on a whole raft of legal and moral responsibilities which were not there when working with volunteers. There is not space in this volume to produce an employment handbook, so I shall need to tackle this differently.

Getting help

The first rule of thumb is to get help. Many ministers have not been involved in employing staff before (depending on their pre-ordination experience) so they should find other people who know what the issues are. There will be business people in most congregations who will know and understand how to go about employing people. The diocesan office will usually have someone who can help and advise. But above all, get help and don't try to wing it! The PCC will usually be the employer, but the minister, as chair, needs to know what is happening and that things are being done properly.

The legal issues

The canons only make mention of two types of employee. Even
then the reference is to appointments, which may also include
appointees who are not employees. The first is the organist or
director of music. There is more on this subject elsewhere,[1] but
note that one significant fact is that the canon is explicit that the
appointment (and any termination of appointment) of an organist must be by the minister and PCC jointly. The minister has no
power to act on his or her own in that regard.[2]

The canons also mention the appointment of a parish clerk,
sexton, verger, or other officer who may be appointed by the minister and the PCC to perform such services upon such terms and
conditions as they may think fit.[3] So any appointment a parish
makes, including employing staff of virtually any sort, is subject
to this and to the law of the land.

This will involve the PCC in ensuring that they implement
good practice. It will be important to explore such things as job
description, person specification, interviewing skills, training,
supervision, employment rights and responsibilities, grievance
procedures, procedures for terminating employment, wages, tax,
and pensions.[4]

Relevant legislation

All this will involve you knowing about a whole range of legislation. This could include the following:

Sex Discrimination Act 1975	Prevents discrimination against people on the ground of gender.
Race Relations Act 1976	Prevents discrimination on the grounds of race.

---

1 See Chapter 15.
2 Canon B20.
3 Canon E3.
4 A good starting point is Behrens, *Practical Church Management*,
chapter 6.

Disability Discrimination Act 2005	Prevents discrimination on the grounds of disability and gives responsibilities to organizations over access and support for the disabled.
Children Act 1989	Governs child protection issues and procedures.
Employment Rights Act 1996	Regulates the rights and responsibilities of employers and employees.
Health and Safety at Work Act 1974	Legislation that ensures that employers assess risk towards employees and take steps accordingly.
Employment Act 2002	Regulates, among other things, what paperwork must be produced for an employee.
Fire Precautions (Workplace) Regulations 1997	Ensures that appropriate fire precautions are in place.
Employment Equality (Sexual Orientation) Regulations 2003	Prevents discrimination on the grounds of sexual orientation, although churches may be able to argue a genuine occupational requirement.
Equality Act 2006	Further regulation on equality that has provision for equal treatment of people regardless of age, disability, gender, race, religion and sexual orientation. There may be occasions when a church is exempt, but the issue needs addressing.
Employment Equality (Religion or Belief) Regulations 2003	Prevents discrimination on the grounds of religion or belief, although churches may be able to argue a genuine occupational requirement.

National Minimum Wage Act 1998	Regulates minimum wage payments.
Employers Liability (Compulsory Insurance) Act 1969	Regulates employer insurance.
Asylum and Immigration Act 1996	Regulates the employment of those from overseas.
Income tax and PAYE legislation and regulations generally	Taxation and social security payments.

Job descriptions

It is important before anyone is employed to have a clear job description. This has two purposes. It helps anyone who is involved in making the appointment to be clear as to what task has been identified. This is useful, especially in churches, as it helps to avoid reshaping the job to match a particular applicant. Sometimes applicants are thin on the ground and other times there are plenty of applicants, but it is important to be clear what task is needed and to stick to this, otherwise you end up employing someone for all the wrong reasons. A job description will also help someone applying for the job, and the person who is employed, to have a clear understanding of what will be expected and what they must do to satisfy the PCC as their employers. It also protects them from unreasonable expectations when all sorts of people think they can tell them what to do.

A job description should contain the name of the job, the place of work, the person to whom the employee is accountable and the frequency of reporting to that person, the key tasks of the job, the names or roles of anyone for whom the employee will be responsible, terms and conditions of the job, reference to CRB checks,[5] training which will be available or expected, and details of how

---

5 See Chapter 20.

the job description and the person's performance in role will be reviewed.

Person specification

In addition to a job description it is useful to have a person specification. This enables those who will be responsible on behalf of the PCC to have a clear idea of the gifts, skills and qualities which will be required in a person employed in the job. It also gives them clear criteria to use when interviewing.

Training

Discipleship and pilgrimage are all about learning and moving on. Just as clergy are expected to be involved in Continuing Ministerial Education, so it is good for a PCC to expect that any staff it employs will have opportunity and funding for development of their work and ministry. A training fund should be built into the budget for any job so that people can develop their skills and grow in their work.

Supervision

Church employees are particularly vulnerable to problems over management and supervision. If the PCC is funding a post from the giving of church members it is easy for any and every member of the church family to think they can have a piece of the employee. This needs to be avoided by establishing clear lines of supervision and reporting. Then, if a problem arises, the church members and the employee know who is the right person to approach.

Employment rights

The PCC will need to very aware of the fact that under the Employment Rights Act 1996, employees have a range of rights which need to be respected. This puts them in a very different position from that of the clergy and it is important for everyone to understand this.

Among other things, an employee is entitled to:

- A statement of employment particulars.[6]
- A pay slip showing how their wages are calculated (tax deductions etc.).[7]
- Time off for maternity, paternity or adoption leave and for ante-natal care.[8]
- Flexible working hours for parents with young or disabled children.[9]
- Sick pay including Statutory Sick Pay.[10]
- A minimum period of notice.[11]
- The right not to be unfairly dismissed.[12]
- A statement setting out reasons if they are dismissed.[13]
- Payments if they are made redundant.[14]

Statement of Particulars of Employment

When a person is employed they are entitled to a Statement of Particulars of Employment, which will set out the terms and conditions that have been agreed to. This must be given within two months of starting work. It should include the following details:

- The name of the employer and the employee.
- The date on which employment began.
- The job title or a brief job description.
- The rate of pay, and dates of payments.
- Normal working hours.
- The place of work.
- Holiday and holiday pay entitlements.

---

6 Employment Rights Act 1996, s1.
7 Employment Rights Act 1996, s8.
8 Employment Rights Act 1996, ss71, 80A, and 55.
9 Employment Rights Act 1996, s80F.
10 Social Security Contributions and Benefits Act 1992.
11 Employment Rights Act 1996, ss86 and 87.
12 Employment Rights Act 1996, s94.
13 Employment Rights Act 1996, s92.
14 Employment Rights Act 1996, s135.

- Sick pay entitlement.
- Pension entitlement.
- Length of notice to be given by either side.
- Disciplinary and grievance procedures.[15]

These details protect both sides from misunderstanding and confusion as to what has been agreed.

Grievance procedures

Sadly sometimes things do go wrong. It is important to have in place a procedure for dealing with this situation so that everyone knows where they stand. There is a statutory grievance procedure and the parish procedure should follow this.[16]

FAQs

Can an employee of the PCC be a PCC member?

Probably not, but it is not entirely clear. See the fuller answer in Chapter 5.[17]

Is all this really necessary? Can't we just let people get on with the job?

It would be lovely to think that the church is above all these things, but it is not. People are entitled to their proper employment rights and the church must take employing people seriously.

Does all this apply to clergy?

No, parish clergy are not employees; they are office holders. New arrangements for the terms of that office are under discussion, which in some ways will mirror what is said here, but will not be

---

15 Employment Rights Act 1996, ss1 and 2.

16 Employment Act 2002, Schedule 2.

17 For a discussion of this issue see *Legal Opinions concerning the Church of England*, p. 139.

subject to the same legislation. It will be called the Ecclesiastical Offices (Terms of Service) Measure.[18]

What happens when ...

... *an employer or an employee wants to end the employment?*

The normal way for termination of employment is for one party or the other to give notice. There are statutory minimum periods for this.[19] If you dismiss someone without giving them the proper notice this is wrongful dismissal and could lead to a claim for damages.

Occasionally it may be that an employee is dismissed following disciplinary procedures. Again there is a standard procedure available for this in the current legislation.[20]

If the PCC is not able to continue funding an employee then it may be that redundancy is necessary. Again, there are procedures to be followed carefully. A person made redundant may, if they have been employed for two years, be entitled to a redundancy payment. Details are again in the Employment Act and on the web-sites referred to at the end of the chapter.[21]

Resources you should have at your fingertips

- Your staff handbook.

- Job description.

- Grievance and disciplinary procedures.

- Health and safety policy.

---

18 See the note in Chapter 11.

19 One week's notice within the first two years, and thereafter one week for each year's continuous employment up to a maximum of twelve weeks. Employment Rights Act 1996, ss86 and 87.

20 Employment Act 2002, Schedule 2.

21 Employment Rights Act 1996, s136.

Useful links

- A useful site setting out all the requirements of employment law is www.emplaw.co.uk

- Other useful government web-sites are: Statutory Sick Pay: www.dwp.gov.uk/lifeevent/benefits/statutory_sick_pay.asp; Inland Revenue: www.hmrc.gov.uk; and generally: www.direct.gov.uk

- Information about the Church Workers Pension Fund is available from http://www.cofe.anglican.org/about/cepb/pensions/cwpf

- There is a lot of useful information at the Methodist Church web-site: go to www.methodist.org.uk then click on Books and Resources, followed by Lay Employment Info.

- John Truscott has a range of useful resources on his web-site at www.john-truscott.co.uk

- The Royal School of Church Musicians has some useful information concerning the employment of organists: www.rscm.com. Contracts for such people are dealt with at www.ism.org

19

Working with Volunteers

A possible scenario

The PCC is due to discuss the rector's new volunteer policy. You have never heard of anything so silly in all your life. Volunteers are volunteers and it is not for the PCC to decide what they will or will not do. The rector should just be grateful for any help he is given. After all, he is paid to do his job but you get nothing. Is this a realistic position to take?

What you need to know

Generally

The term 'volunteers' is very wide. It can refer to a range of people including readers,[1] churchwardens[2] and treasurers.[3] They are all volunteers but require special attention, and are discussed elsewhere in this work. This chapter is more general, as it is about almost everyone involved in the church.

With the exception of paid clergy and any other employees, all church members are volunteers. This means that they are free to come and go as they please. The incumbent in a parish has a special status, as he or she has been called by God to be the leader of the parish and its ministry, but that authority is not something to be flaunted. I usually say to clergy when I am training them: you have no authority in the church except that which you earn.

There are a few other offices in the Church of England which

---

1 Chapter 12.
2 Chapter 3.
3 Chapter 16.

the canons mention, such as sidesmen,[4] and officers of the PCC,[5] but generally the church is run by volunteers who are not mentioned in the canons. How then does a church go about setting appropriate boundaries with such people? There is much material available on this subject, usually under the heading 'voluntary sector', and the Church of England can learn good practice in this area from this material. What follows is some advice about working with volunteers and particularly the legal issues that affect volunteers.

The legal status of volunteers

The legal position of volunteers is not a straightforward issue. Volunteers are not included in most legislation concerning the workplace. This means that they are not protected by the anti-discrimination legislation, and do not have access to employment rights. Legislation around criminal record checks when working with children and vulnerable people does include volunteers, as it refers to the role that a person is in rather than their employment status.[6] Volunteers retain rights we all share as citizens, so, for example, the Data Protection Act applies to personal information kept on them.[7]

Volunteer Policy

Many voluntary organizations have a Volunteer Policy. This is a statement setting out how they will deal with people who work for the organization in a voluntary capacity. It may seem a strange thing for a church to have, but it does force the PCC to think through what it is doing with people and encourage consistent good practice. It might include statements about how the church will go about recruitment and selection for posts, induction and training, expenses, supervision and support, equal opportunities issues and health and safety.

---

4 Canon E2.
5 Church Representation Rules.
6 See Chapter 20.
7 See Chapter 22.

Job descriptions

Whenever a person takes on a voluntary role it is useful for there to be some clear description of what is being asked and agreed to. One of the greatest disincentives which stops people from volunteering is the feeling that they are about to take on a job they don't understand and may be lumbered with for life. A job description or voluntary work agreement (it can be called all sorts of things) sets out the expectations clearly. I always build into such documents clear statements as to who is responsible for the role, what it entails, who has oversight, what support will be available, whether expenses are available, how long the agreement is for and when it will be renewed. I have found it particularly useful always to make such agreements for a two-year period. This is long enough for someone to make a fair stab at the job, but gives a clear end-point. If all is well someone may continue for a further period thereafter, but at least there are regular exit points. The two-year point also gives a chance for review and an opportunity to offer further training and support.

Expenses

Churches have not always had a culture of reimbursing expenses. This is in part because many people would not wish to claim them, as they see their ministry as part of their Christian duty. However, it is appropriate for a PCC to make the offer of reimbursing reasonable expenses for those who take a formal role for the church, and if the person does not wish to claim they can either simply not do so, or claim and then 'gift aid' the expenses back to the church.

PCCs should ensure that when expenses are paid, they reimburse out-of-pocket expenses only. Flat-rate expenses payments, or indeed any sum over and above actual expenses, are likely to be seen as income from the point of view of benefits and tax, and could change the legal status of volunteers to that of employees. Volunteers on benefits may lose part of their benefit if they are seen to have received income, and in any case are likely to be treated as if they are in part-time work rather than volunteering.

Benefits

Volunteering should not affect a person's benefits, as long as they continue to meet the requirements for their particular benefit, and so long as it is clearly genuine voluntary work. Claimants on Job-seeker's Allowance must be available for and actively seeking work. Volunteers must be available to attend interviews at 48 hours' no-tice and start work at one week's notice. This is actually a conces-sion to volunteers from the normal 24 hours' notice. To be actively seeking work, volunteers must continue to take steps to look for work each week (such steps are normally outlined in a Jobseeker's Agreement). The Incapacity Benefit rules regard volunteering as an exempt category of work. It is of course important to avoid volunteers carrying out activities which seem to contradict their reason for being on the benefit, but apart from that, voluntary work should not affect their claim to be incapable of work. Other benefits such as Income Support, Disability Living Allowance, Housing Benefit, etc. should not be affected by volunteering.

Young volunteers

While there are legal restrictions on employing young people, they do not apply to volunteers. It is worth being aware of the legislation, even if you are not bound by it, and to remember that young people have other demands on their time outside volunteer-ing, such as homework, socializing and so on.[8] So far as young volunteers in the church are concerned, the issue often arises over assistance in other children's and young people's groups. No per-son under 18 should ever be left in charge of other children un-der 18. Parental consent should be sought when involving young volunteers. Parental responsibility continues until the age of 18, unless the young person is 16 or older and marries, or is living

---

8 Children and Young Persons Act 1933, s18 and subsequent amend-ments limit employment to those aged 13 or over. It states that no child under minimum school-leaving age may be employed before 7 am or after 7 pm on any day or for more than two hours on any school day or Sunday. The legislation also requires that children must have a minimum of two weeks free from work during the school holidays.

independently. Both the young person and their parent or guardian should fully understand what the voluntary work entails.

Volunteer drivers

Drivers using their own vehicles for church work should inform their insurers of their voluntary activities. To avoid confusion with commercial use of the vehicle, they should make it clear that they will receive out-of-pocket expenses only. This should not result in an increase in premium, as volunteering should be regarded as part of the 'social, domestic and pleasure' use of the vehicle (some insurers may categorize volunteering as a business use, but should not raise the premium). Volunteer drivers should not accept an increase in premium, and may wish to change insurer if their current one insists on an extra charge. PCCs who ask people to use their cars to transport others for church purposes should make sure that volunteers have informed their insurers of their volunteer driving.

HM Customs and Revenue sets a tax-free approved mileage rate for reimbursing travel expenses for people using their own vehicles for volunteering or employment. These can be obtained from HM Customs and Revenue. The rates at the time of writing (for 2008) are:

- Cars and vans: 40p per mile for the first 10,000 miles, and 25p for every mile thereafter.
- Motorcycles: 24p per mile regardless of overall total.
- Bicycles: 20p per mile, again, regardless of overall total.

Reimbursement at levels above these rates is likely to affect the tax status of the volunteers and may have implications for volunteers who are taxpayers or on benefits. For further information on this issue contact your diocesan finance department.

Honoraria

An honorarium is generally understood to be a one-off, unexpected payment given as a gesture of thanks. If a payment is regularly made, or expected (either by the recipient being told of it in advance, or it being common practice to make the payment), then it will no longer be regarded as an honorarium, and will be treated as any other payment to volunteers. There are no clear legal rules on what is or is not an honorarium, and it is not always a helpful way of saying thank you to someone.

FAQs

How can we reward volunteers?

As has been stated above, honoraria may be subject to tax and can cause difficulties. This should not prevent churches from thinking in terms of rewarding volunteers. One of the most neglected mechanisms is to say thank you! It can be easy to forget the obvious. Another way, very appropriate to the church, is to have a celebration and commissioning service, which acknowledges work which has been done (after all, in the church a volunteer is a minister of the gospel) and gives chance for the whole congregation to pray for the ministry of volunteers. Another simple mechanism is to make sure that you keep your volunteers well fed and watered. Having food and snacks available sends the message that your volunteers are noticed and appreciated. A Christmas lunch or summer barbecue will send the same message of gratitude. It's just a case of looking for simple, non-financial ways of saying to those who volunteer that they are appreciated, without getting embroiled in issues over tax and finance.

What are reasonable expenses?

Expenses must be a reimbursement of actual expenditure which must usually be supported by receipts or vouchers. Typical expenses may include (but not necessarily be restricted to):

- Agreed mileage expenses.
- Post and phone costs.
- Stationery costs.
- Purchase of particular items for the task (although it's always better for anything to be bought direct by the PCC if possible).

How can we sack a volunteer?

This usually shows a lack of forward planning. If no job description or agreed expectation is in place, it is possible for the situation to arise where someone thinks the job is indeed theirs for life. Ultimately the minister or churchwardens have no choice but to the grasp the nettle and ask someone to let go of a role, so that others may take it on. This is not always as easy as it sounds.

What happens when ...

... a church wants to make a public collection?

Occasionally a church may consider making house-to-house collections or street collections. These are both subject to regulation.[9] Where this is in the name of a large charity such as Christian Aid, they will have taken the steps to get necessary permissions, but if you do it as a parish project it's down to you. House-to-house collections must be for a charitable purpose and be licensed by the relevant licensing authority. This would normally be the local authority.[10] Collectors must be over the age of 16 and be 'fit and proper persons'. They should be issued with a badge and a certificate of authority, both of which should be signed. The certificate of authority must be produced if either a police officer or a person from whom the collector is asking donations asks to see it. The badge must be worn where it can be clearly seen while collecting.[11]

Street collections are regulated in a different way from house-to-house collections, in that they are not covered by compulsory central regulation. Churches considering street collections should, therefore, seek advice directly from the local licensing authority.[12]

---

9 House-to-house collections come under the House to House Collections Act 1939 and subsequent regulations, while street collections are covered by the Police, Factories etc. (Miscellaneous Provisions) Act 1916 and related regulations.

10 Apart from the Metropolitan Police District in London, where the police commissioner is responsible for licensing, and the City of London, where the Corporation of London's Common Council is the licensing body.

11 House to House Collections Act 1939, s4.

12 As in footnote 9 above.

Resources you should have at your fingertips

- Volunteer Policy.
- Health and Safety Policy.

Useful links

- John Truscott has been a church consultant for many years. His web-site has lots of useful material on it: www.john-truscott. co.uk

- Volunteer England is an organization dealing with the issues of volunteers: www.volunteering.org.uk

- The Methodist Church web-site also has some particularly useful material: www.methodist.org.uk (check for more ideas).

- Further information on house-to-house collections and street collections is available from www.institute-of-fundraising. org.uk

20

Children

A possible scenario

Miss Smith has led the Sunday School in your small church for many years. Most of the time she leads it by herself as it is hard to find volunteers. Recently Mr Brown has started coming to church and he has offered to help, which is very good news. Although he seems like an odd soul in many ways, you wisely visit him in his temporary bed-sit and he assures you that he has had lots of experience with children. This puts your mind at rest. Is there anything else you should consider?

What you need to know

Generally

The Church of England has always taken seriously its responsibility to children and young people. Indeed much of the educational and social system of our country as we now know it derives from this part of the church's ministry. The canons make it a duty for every minister to instruct and teach children in the doctrine, sacraments and discipline of the church as they are set out in Holy Scripture.[1] It is also an obligation on clergy to take up opportunities to visit and teach in the schools of the parish.[2] Parents are required in the canons to ensure that their children are taught in the faith.[3]

---

1 Canon B26(1).
2 Canon C24(4).
3 Canon B26(2).

It is important not to lose sight of these requirements, as much of what follows focuses on the framework within which such work takes place today. The Children Act 1989 places obligations on everyone who is involved in working with children, and therefore has significant impact on the churches' work in this area. This chapter will explore some of the issues raised by that Act.

Principles

The rules about working with children in churches are not just based on the legislation alone but on theology and a set of principles set out by the House of Bishops in their policy document.[4] The theological statement concludes with the following:

> A Christian approach to child protection will therefore ask both individuals and communities to create a safe environment for children and young people, to act promptly on any complaints made, to care for those who have been abused in the past, and to minister appropriately to those who have abused.

The principles which follow on from this are:

- We are committed to the safeguarding, care and nurture of the children within our church community.
- We will carefully select and train ordained and lay ministers, volunteers and paid workers with children and young people, using the Criminal Records Bureau, among other tools, to check the background of each person.
- We will respond without delay to every complaint made, that a child or young person for whom we are responsible may have been harmed.
- We will fully co-operate with statutory agencies during any investigation they make into allegations concerning a member of the church community.
- We will seek to offer informed pastoral care to any child, young person or adult who has suffered abuse.

---

4 *Protecting All God's Children*, the Church of England Child Protection Policy (3rd edn).

- We will care for and supervise any member of our church community known to have offended against a child and their families where appropriate.[5]

Child protection policy

There is a House of Bishops' Policy on Child Protection, and every diocese has also adopted such a policy. It is a responsibility on every parish also to have such a policy. A minister and a PCC should ensure that a policy is in place that reflects the diocesan policy. Each diocese has a Diocesan Child Protection Adviser (DCPA) who should offer training and help in this.

PCC responsibilities

Every parish[6] has certain responsibilities as set out in the national guidelines. They should:

- Accept the prime duty of care placed upon the incumbent and PCC to ensure the well-being of children and young people in the church community.
- Adopt and implement a child protection policy and procedure, accepting as a minimum the House of Bishops' Policy on Child Protection, but informed by additional diocesan procedures and recommended good practice, while being responsive to local parish requirements.
- Appoint someone as Child Protection Officer to work with the incumbent and the PCC to implement policy and procedures. This person must ensure that any concerns about a child or the behaviour of an adult are appropriately reported, both to the statutory agencies and to the diocesan child protection adviser. Ideally this named person should be someone without other pastoral responsibility for children in the parish.
- Appoint a person, who may be different from the co-ordinator,

---

5 *Protecting All God's Children*, p. 6.
6 This means the minister and the PCC who together have responsibility in this area.

to be a children's advocate; this should be someone children know they could talk to about any problems, if they so wish.
- Display the Childline telephone number.
- Ensure that all those authorized to work with children and young people or in a position of authority are appropriately appointed, trained and supported, and provide all authorized personnel with a copy of the parish child protection policy, procedures and good practice guidelines.
- Pay particular attention to children with special needs and those from ethnic minorities to ensure their full integration and protection within the church community.
- Ensure that appropriate pastoral care is available for those adults who have disclosed that they have been abused as children.
- Provide, as appropriate, support for all parents and families in the congregation, being aware particularly of parents whose children have suffered abuse.
- Ensure that those who may pose a threat to children and young people are effectively managed and monitored.
- Ensure that appropriate health and safety policies and procedures are in place.
- Provide appropriate insurance cover for all activities undertaken in the name of the parish, and ensure that the PCC has approved all activities involving children for insurance purposes.
- Review the implementation of the child protection policy, procedures and good practice, at least annually.[7]

Child Protection Officer

Every parish must appoint a Child Protection Officer (CPO). This should be someone who will take responsibility for ensuring that the diocesan and parish policies are put into practice and followed. It may be useful for such a person to have a professional background in working with children, such as a teacher, health visitor, or social worker. This is not a requirement, but will enable them more quickly to get to grips with the issues involved.

---

7 *Protecting All God's Children*, p. 8.

It may also be helpful if they are someone without other pastoral responsibility for children in the parish. This enables them to have an uncompromised passion for seeing that the obligations are fulfilled. The diocese usually offers training to parish CPOs and if this involves a cost the PCC should be willing to pay.

The tasks of the CPO are to:

- Ensure that the Parish Child Protection Policy is in place, up to date and followed.
- Advise the PCC about child protection matters.
- Be a point of contact for anyone with concerns about children or adults in the parish.
- Organize Criminal Record Bureau checks for all existing and new leaders.
- Be a link between the parish and the Diocesan Child Protection Adviser.
- Arrange training on child protection matters for all involved in the parish.
- Assist in health and safety risk assessments.[8]
- Make a report to the PCC at least once each year.[9]

Criminal Record Bureau (CRB)

All people who have involvement with children should be checked with the CRB. This can often be more than first meets the eye. There are, of course, the clergy, readers, all authorized ministers of the church, the Sunday School leaders and youth workers, any employee of the church in any capacity, anyone involved in any crèche or in a capacity of any sort which includes the supervision of children, anyone whose role in the church means that they are known by the children and young people as a responsible adult, and anyone involved in summer holiday clubs or short-term projects. The list could go on. The rule of thumb I use in a parish is: is this person someone a child might approach in the street and say, 'That's Mr/Mrs X from church; I can trust them'? If so, they should be checked.

---

8 See Chapter 21.
9 Behrens, *Practical Church Management*, p. 150.

The CPO will receive information and instructions from the diocesan adviser as to how to go about making CRB checks. Broadly speaking a CRB check involves filling in a form and providing proof of identification and references. The forms are forwarded by the CPO to the diocesan adviser who will in turn forward then to the CRB. If the return is not clear the diocesan adviser will guide the CPO or minister as to whether it is appropriate for that person to take up a post in the parish and if so on what terms.

Training

The CPO will need to ensure that other people involved in the parish are aware of the parish policy and its meaning.[10] This may involve setting up local training or encouraging others to attend a diocesan training course. Copies of the parish policy should be given to everyone who is working with children and to all PCC members and displayed in the parish.

Appointments

It does not always sit comfortably with church members to be asked for references and CRB checks when they volunteer. It seems to cut against a culture of trust and honesty which ought to be part of church life. However, those responsible for making appointments in the name of the church have a duty to be sure that they have done all they can. Indeed, it is an offence to recruit anyone to work with children or vulnerable adults who is an offender or otherwise disqualified from such work.[11]

In order to ensure that the parish has taken proper steps to protect children and volunteers alike, the following steps should be followed for prospective appointees (paid or voluntary):

- Make sure that the role someone is offering to fulfil is defined in writing.

---

10 *Protecting All God's Children*, p. 9.
11 Criminal Justice and Court Services Act 2000, s35.

- Ask people to complete an application form.
- Take up references.
- Get people to complete a 'Confidential Declaration' form. This asks them whether they have any previous convictions or cautions which might make them unsuitable to work with children.
- Make a CRB check at the appropriate level.
- Offer the post subject to a probationary period.
- Confirm the appointment in writing.
- Ensure that all appointees have a copy of the parish child protection policy.
- Commission people for their role so that everyone in the church knows.[12]

Culture

One of the responsibilities of the PCC is to create a culture of informed vigilance which takes children and young people seriously. It may not be obvious what that means. It includes the following:

- Raising awareness of the issues involved in protecting children and young people in the church.
- Addressing the needs of our children and young people in all their cultural, spiritual, intellectual, racial and physical diversity.
- Responding to the needs of children, young people and adults who have been abused.
- Supporting and training those who work with children and young people, encouraging them to work together to follow good practice.
- Caring appropriately for those in the church community who have abused children.[13]

---

12 *Protecting All God's Children*, p. 45.
13 *Protecting All God's Children*, p. 6.

Review

It is always tempting to think we have finished a task of this sort, but it is important that the parish child protection policy and practice is kept under review. Annually the CPO should check that the policy is still up to date and in step with the diocesan policy and whether any changes need to be made. This will ensure that the parish does not lag behind.[14]

Role of clergy

Clergy share in the responsibility of the PCC to ensure that good child protection practice is followed in the parish. In addition there is a variety of ways in which a member of the clergy may become involved pastorally with issues involving child protection. It may be that a parishioner will approach a minister for help on discovering that their child has been abused. Possibly a child in a school will confide in the minister. A youth group leader may express concerns regarding a child in the group, or perhaps an allegation of abuse will be made against a member of the congregation.

In these situations, the minister will often feel exposed and vulnerable. There are many theological and pastoral questions to be asked. What support can be expected? How can a victim and the accused both be cared for by the church? What about the families of both? What relationship should a minister have with other agencies, and which agencies? How does this situation relate to the minister's theology? What does it say about sin, forgiveness, justice? What about other people in the congregation?

The minister's first instinct might be to try to ignore the whole thing and hope it goes away. This is not an option. The first and most important thing to realize is that no one is expected to deal with such situations on their own, even though confidentiality is a central part of their role. The Diocesan Child Protection Adviser (DCPA) is there specifically to offer guidance, support and expertise, and has contact with the statutory services. Get help quickly and act wisely.

---

14 *Protecting All God's Children*, p. 9.

Conflicts of interest

It is right to recognize that there will be conflicts of interest in these complex issues, especially if allegations are made. It may be that a church wants to offer support to people who have experienced child abuse in the past, to manage the risk of a perpetrator of abuse becoming a member of the church, and to keep children safe in the church. This will not be easy. It is very easy to become entangled in the complexities of such a situation and it is well known that perpetrators can be very skilled in manipulation. Managing such a complex situation needs to involve the minister and the CPO eliciting additional support, for example from the DCPA, or from other local clergy who could perhaps offer pastoral care to the family of the alleged abuser, while someone else concentrates on the care of the family and the victim of the alleged abuser.

Working with the community

Clergy and parishes have not always been good at seeing their work in the context of the wider community. We need to learn to work not only with those within the wider church but also within the community. Clergy could seek to network more widely with other local agencies: GPs, police, social workers, etc. Some do this more naturally than others. Such networking will not only make the work of child protection much easier, but it will achieve a shift in the perceptions which others hold of the church.

Health and safety

Part of keeping children safe is to have a health and safety policy in a church. This is likely to cover a whole range of subjects which are about keeping everyone, not only children, safe and free from foreseeable harm. For more on this subject see Chapter 21.

Independent Safeguarding Authority

From autumn 2008 a new agency will be established by the above name. This body will keep a register of all who have had

CRB checks and who work with children (and other vulnerable people). They will be bringing together information currently held by a range of agencies so that safeguarding is dealt with in a coherent way. This will involve some changes in procedures, and diocesan advisers will assist parishes in the new processes as they come on line.

FAQs

What 'leader-to-child ratio' should we have in our children's work?

At no time should children be left in the care of one adult alone. It is unsafe for the children and for the adult. Indeed best practice would suggest that it is not just a case of not leaving one person alone, but rather of usually having *at least* two and usually more. The national guideline sets out a guide to leader-to-child ratios as follows:

For 0–2 years   1 leader to every 3 children
For 2–3 years   1 leader to every 4 children
For 3–8 years   1 leader to every 8 children[15]

Some dioceses offer even more careful ratios, so check your diocesan policy. These suggestions are not just there to try to scupper your plans. They are to help you. Suppose a child is hurt and needs attention, who is going to look after the others? Or, suppose an allegation is made against one of the leaders that something inappropriate happened? Who will know whether it happened or not if only one person was present? You do not have to be able to find lots of people who can teach your Sunday School, for example. There may only be one person with the gifts to be a Sunday School teacher, but there may well be others who can be checked and then take a turn to 'sit in'. That is fine.

---

15 *Children Act 1989 – Guidance and Regulations*, published in 1997.

What if I suspect something has happened or I am suspicious about someone?

It is always wise to have a conversation straight away with the DCPA. Most clergy, churchwardens and PCC members are very unfamiliar with this territory and you will need all the help and wise advice you can get.[16]

When must I report?

There is a lot of helpful advice about this issue in the national policy document.[17] The guidelines state that any disclosure made by a child about abuse must be reported to social services immediately. It is not for you to establish the facts – that is for the police and social services.

Therefore, it is vital that you do not question either the child or the alleged abuser. The DCPA can provide valuable support at such times; in particular giving moral support when contact is made with other agencies. Just like the clergy, other agencies have concerns about confidentiality and, as with the church, they have sometimes overstated the 'need to know factor'. This has meant that the contribution of churches in the area of child protection has sometimes been neglected. Just as the church has acknowledged the role of other agencies, so too the police, probation and social services have recognized that churches have significant contact with, and care of, children.

What records need to be kept?

There are two matters to mention here. The first is that there must be a proper procedure for keeping the confidential declaration forms in the parish and the child protection paperwork. My own practice has been that the former came to me as incumbent and I kept them. The CPO then only dealt with the CRB paperwork, which seemed to work well.

---

16 *Protecting All God's Children*, p. 27.
17 *Protecting All God's Children*, p. 19.

The second issue relates to any situation where a rumour, allegation or concern arises. In such circumstances it is sensible for anyone involved to keep a written record and to sign and date it. If any later changes are made to the note these should also be signed and dated. Then, if at a later date your concerns are taken further in some way, you know what you thought and said at the time. The following is useful advice about keeping any such notes:

- there should be a signature and date;
- the name of the signatory should be clearly identified;
- information should be factual, accurate, and clear;
- notes should be stored in a safe place to ensure confidentiality;
- notes should be written as if the person was looking over your shoulder;
- only record information necessary for the purpose;
- distinguish facts from opinions;
- distinguish personal values;
- be concrete and specific rather than abstract and generalized;
- use simple language;
- emphasize strengths and positive steps that can be taken to improve a situation, rather than labelling the person and their world;
- make recording a part of normal practice.[18]

What happens if a known perpetrator wants to join our church?

It is possible that someone who has a history as a perpetrator might want to join a church. Clearly the gospel is meant for everyone, not just children and non-offending adults. How should a minister or CPO react and what steps should be taken to protect everyone? The procedures below should be followed:[19]

- The minister informs the DCPA.
- The DCPA advises the statutory agencies and seeks guidance.

---

18 This advice is based on the Diocese of Chelmsford policy.

19 This advice is based on the Diocese of Chelmsford policy: you should check out your own diocesan policy to be sure.

- The DCPA attends a risk management meeting, if appropriate, or co-ordinates a meeting with key personnel in the parish (the DCPA will advise who should attend according to the circumstances).
- Information is shared as appropriate.
- This is analysed, and guidance and advice offered.

The perpetrator will be made aware that this process is taking place. In respect of a perpetrator joining a parish, consideration will be given by the group referred to above as to:

- Who needs to know within the congregation.
- How the person might be introduced within the congregation.
- What child protection agreement should be established with the person.
- Who should be responsible for ensuring compliance with this plan.
- If there is a failure of compliance, what sanctions should be imposed, and how.
- Which named person in the police, probation and social services will be available for future guidance and advice, and for referring of concerns and any new information.
- How the parish can effectively support the person in ways which encourage them not to re-offend.
- What are the time and physical boundary constraints.

Actions are agreed and roles and responsibilities established between the minister, the perpetrator and the DCPA. Actions are implemented within the parish by the minister, who will be able to liaise with the DCPA throughout. Regular reviews should take place with the DCPA. Representatives in the statutory agencies will advise the DCPA if any pertinent information comes to light concerning the perpetrator, which is relevant to his or her involvement in the parish.[20]
There is also information in diocesan policies concerning steps to be taken if the person then moves on from the parish to another place.

---

20 *Protecting All God's Children*, p. 41.

We are a small rural parish with few resources. Do we need to do all this?

Yes, you do. Rural parishes or parishes held in plurality may wish to join together to implement the policy and procedures. This may be a good use of resources and ensure that child protection matters are dealt with properly. It is perfectly proper for a number of PCCs to share a policy and a CPO so long as each PCC approves the arrangement to fulfil its obligations. Sometimes people imagine that the rural church is a safe place and has few children to worry about anyway. It should be noted, however, that people working in isolated situations can be vulnerable, and care should be taken to implement the policy in full.[21]

We are part of a local ecumenical project. How does it work for us?

Local ecumenical projects should agree which denomination's child protection policy to follow, and this decision should be ratified by the bishop and other appropriate church leaders. This will ensure that there is no ambiguity. Most of the major denominations have similar procedures, but so long as it is clear which one you are working to, you will not go far wrong.[22]

What happens when ...

... someone makes an admission in the confessional?

First it is important to point out that this question and the answer is very specific. It relates only to the formal sacrament of confession, and not to other pastoral conversations. The House of Bishops advises that the 'seal of the confessional' should be regarded as absolute; that is, the information should not be passed on to anyone.[23] However, this may not be consistent with civil

---

21 *Protecting All God's Children*, p. 9.

22 *Protecting All God's Children*, p. 9.

23 See Proviso to Canon 113 of the Canons of 1603 printed in the Supplementary Material at the back of the Canons.

law. The best advice at present is to urge the person to report their behaviour to the police or social services, and to withhold absolution until this has been done.[24]

... *other people use our premises?*

Generally the PCC must make sure that it has fulfilled its own responsibilities, and others must do the same. It would seem to be good practice to ask, as part of any hall-booking procedure, whether the incoming group will have any involvement with children, and whether they have a child protection policy and have undertaken CRB checks. If the answer to this question is yes, then the PCC has probably taken its own responsibility sufficiently. If they do not have a policy, you may want to ask more and even encourage them to get one. It might be appropriate to consider whether the PCC wishes to continue with the booking if no policy is put in place within a fixed period, say six months. While the policy is the responsibility of the person using the hall, the PCC may properly be concerned if no such policy and CRB checks are in place and may feel it right to take a firm line to ensure good practice, even when the responsibility ultimately lies elsewhere.

Resources you should have at your fingertips

- House of Bishops' Child Protection Policy *Protecting All God's Children*.

- Diocesan Child Protection Policy.

- Parish Policy.

Useful links

- The national policy is available at www.cofe.anglican.org/info/papers/protectingchildren.pdf

---

24 *Protecting All God's Children*, p. 20. There is a fuller discussion as to the legal nature of confidentiality in *Legal Opinions concerning the Church of England*, p. 43ff.

- Every diocese should have a diocesan child protection policy. You need to know what your own diocesan policy says. Many are available on-line, but if you need some quick advice and can't get to your own diocesan version, try www.chelmsford. anglican.org for an excellent example. It runs to 248 pages and covers all the ground fully.

- Government advice on child protection matters at www. everychildmatters.gov.uk

- Information on the Criminal Records Bureau and the disclosure process at www.crb.gov.uk

- Childline provides a service to those (especially children) who feel they need a listening ear: 0800 1111 (open 24 hours), www. childline.org.uk

21

Health and Safety

A possible scenario

James is employed by the church as a handyman and to do church-yard maintenance. In early December he is greeted by the vicar in the churchyard while he is putting up the Christmas lights. 'Mind you don't slip on that ladder', says the vicar. 'I've been doing this task for 18 years and I've never fallen off yet', came the joking reply. An hour later they are laughing together about the exchange as they wait in A & E for James to have his shoulder x-rayed. What are the implications for the PCC?

What you need to know

Employees and volunteers

Churches, like any organization, have a legal responsibility towards their employees[1] and volunteers.[2] In practice this means taking all reasonable steps to prevent harm coming to them, either through action or inaction. Health and safety issues for churches are not just a matter of good practice, but a requirement of the law.

On the whole, churches have not been good at thinking about health and safety issues. PCCs need to be aware that when they allow clergy, employees, volunteers and visitors to come onto the premises they have a responsibility to ensure that they are safe. At a number of points already in this book I have mentioned this subject in passing, and this chapter is intended to give some guidance.

---

1 Health and Safety at Work etc. Act 1974, s2.
2 Health and Safety at Work etc. Act 1974, s3 and 4.

If you are new to health and safety, it can be hard to decide exactly where to start in your church. The number of topics and the issues that need to be considered can seem bewildering, but with a little time and planning it is perfectly possible to get on top of the subject.

Health and safety is about reducing the chance of someone being harmed. It is not about eliminating risk, but controlling it. Risk assessment is central to health and safety and is a requirement of the law.[3] Risk assessment should be used in every stage of the process in one form or another. Churches vary in size, from small to very large, from a single room to a large building with many rooms. The people who use the premises could be very young, very old, disabled or have other needs that should be taken into consideration. Every situation is different and the needs of every congregation vary.

Getting started

The following is a guideline on how to begin the process in your own church. Start by planning. Perhaps the PCC has someone who has a background knowledge of this subject who could take a lead for you. If not, set up a small group which can take a look at the issues and report to the PCC. This would usually be about six people who should reflect the mix of people and activities in your church, and could include external users.

Do an initial review of the premises. Look at the various parts of your church and how they are used. Who uses them? What are they used for? Start to list things as you notice them and then you will build up a picture of issues to address.

Next make a plan to help to correct as many of the items from the initial review as possible. Some items will need immediate action while others can be put off for some time (but not for ever!). Prioritize things as high, medium and low risks, so that you can do things in the best order. You will probably make quite a lot of progress on small things just for having started the process.

---

3 The Management of Health and Safety at Work Regulations 1999, regulation 3.

As time goes on you will be able to do a more thorough and complete risk assessment. This may involve writing a health and safety policy.[4] Discuss any issues with others who use the building – members of your congregation, such as a choirmaster, who might lead a group, or people from outside groups that use the building. Let them know what you are doing and ask them if they have any issues they would like to see addressed.

Review the situation regularly and keep working at it. It is like maintaining a historic church building or painting the Forth Bridge. It is not a task to finish, but to go on doing.

An initial review

An initial review will bring to light some of the most obvious things. Consider these starter questions:

- Is there a first aid kit and are the contents in date? Do people know where it is?
- Do you have fire extinguishers? Are they serviced?
- Do you have a fire alarm and is it tested regularly?
- Are there any hazards or issues you know about?
- Is there anything that has caused an accident, fire or near-miss in the last twelve months?

This might bring to light any obvious things which should urgently be put to rights.

Basic equipment you must have

The basic equipment needed in every church includes:

1 A first aid kit and an accident book.[5]
2 Fire extinguishers.[6]
3 Exit signs.[7]

---

4 A policy is obligatory for an organization with five or more employees. Health and Safety at Work etc. Act 1974, s2(3).

5 Health and Safety (First Aid) Regulations 1981.

6 Regulatory Reform (Fire Safety) Order 2005, Article 13.

7 Regulatory Reform (Fire Safety) Order 2005, Article 14.

4 Health and Safety Law poster.[8]
5 Health and Safety Policy Statement.[9]
6 Fire action poster.[10]

These are not all things which churches have seen as necessary in the past but they should be there.

Risk assessment

As your group starts to work on the issue they will deal quickly with the basics and start to look more closely at the building. It is important now to start to decide what the health and safety risks are. This is called risk assessment. It allows you to decide what could cause harm to people in your church. Treat it as a fact-finding exercise which can then be used to help you reduce the risks in the building.

The simplest form is known as the 'Five Steps' method, which is perfectly adequate for use by churches.[11] The Five Steps are:

Step 1 Identify the hazards   Hazards can include items that could cause someone to slip, trip or fall, things that get hot that could burn, electrical hazards and hazards from equipment such as display screens. Look around the building to find those things that you consider a significant hazard. You need to look in parts of the premises you don't often use such as boiler rooms, store rooms and towers as well as the parts of the building you use regularly. Look outside the building and see if there are any hazards that could affect people, including members of the public. It is easy to overlook some hazards because they are familiar. Try to look with fresh and critical eyes. It is also useful to ask people who use the premises if they know of anything that they consider to be a significant hazard.

---

8 Health and Safety (Information for Employees) Regulations 1989, regulation 4. This applies when a church has employees.

9 Health and Safety at Work etc. Act 1974, s2(3).

10 Regulatory Reform (Fire Safety) Order 2005, Article 19.

11 Based on an advisory leaflet from the Health and Safety Executive web-site.

Step 2 Decide who might be harmed and how Consider the people who use the building and how the hazard could affect them. While some parts of the building might be open to the public on a regular basis, other areas might only be used by one or two people on an occasional basis. Consider the needs of disabled people and the elderly. Also, take into consideration things that could pose a significant risk to young children or babies. People such as church sitters and caretakers usually work by themselves, so consider these people as being at significant risk.

Step 3 Evaluate the risks and decide on precautions Risk is the chance that someone could be harmed. It is useful to categorize risks as 'low', 'medium' or 'high' for convenience. As a guide, 'low' risks do not need any significant attention (but do not rule out making any improvements). 'Medium' risks need some attention to try to bring them to a 'low' level. 'High' risks should be prioritized as needing improvement to bring them down to a 'low' level. Be honest and don't try to minimize the risk assessment outcome for convenience or to hide any problems. The additional measures you put into place need not be complex. Most of the time it is just a case of making some simple changes that should not cost anything. You might need to purchase some items but these should not be too expensive for most churches.

Step 4 Record your findings and implement them Risk assessment is a legal requirement[12] and in all cases it is recommended. You might need to prove that you have done a risk assessment in the future. The risk assessments should be dated and preferably signed, then filed somewhere safe for future reference. The risk assessments would be used when writing a health and safety policy and you should refer to them regularly.

Step 5 Review your risk assessment and update if necessary Risk assessments should be reviewed occasionally to ensure that they remain valid. For most places of worship, a review every 12 months should be adequate. If you have never done a

---

12 The Management of Health and Safety at Work Regulations 1999, regulation 3.

risk assessment before, it is a good idea to review them in about six months' time as you are likely to be more able to spot hazards and make a judgement about the risk. Each time you review and revise your risk assessment, you are likely to identify new hazards, think of new control measures and make further improvements. Always aim to make improvements. [13]

Health and safety policy

One way in which you can show that you are taking health and safety seriously is to have a health and safety policy as a PCC. It is an obligation if you employ over five people.[14] It need not be over-complicated but it will show your commitment to get these things right. Such a policy might start with a general statement of commitment to the issue. This could be followed by commitments to do regular risk assessments, maintain equipment, and to offer staff and volunteers training and supervision in health and safety matters. The policy should state who is responsible for health and safety matters and who to contact over any concerns. It can then cover any specific issues relevant to your church. You can find suitable examples on the Internet to get you going.[15]

Disability discrimination and accessibility

There is also a legal requirement[16] for churches to be accessible. Churches must take reasonable measures to ensure access for those who are disabled. This includes making adjustments to buildings and facilities. There are many different disabilities and some are more obvious than others. You might not even be aware that someone has a disability in your congregation. Additionally, some people might have impaired mobility (including some elderly people) and the measures and aids you put into place could

---

13 The HSE web-site has these principles and they are usefully expanded with reference to churches on the ChurchSafety web-site.

14 Health and Safety at Work etc. Act 1974, s2(3). There is a draft policy on the Ecclesiastical Insurance web-site.

15 There is a draft policy on the Ecclesiastical Insurance web-site.

16 Disability Discrimination Act 1995.

be of use to these people also. The reasonableness test[17] means that you will not be forced into a major project you can't afford, but part of health and safety is to ensure that you have taken disability issues seriously. It is good practice to discuss any measures that are to be deferred on the basis of cost in the PCC and to ensure that a proper minute is taken.

Food safety and hygiene

Many churches have a kitchen and handle food, whether that is on a routine basis preparing daily meals or an annual fundraising event. The same basic food safety rules apply to all situations.[18] These include:

- Kitchens should be well lit and ventilated.
- They should have enough space for there to be different food preparation areas to keep raw food from pre-prepared food.
- They must have a hand-washing sink which is supplied with hot and cold running water.
- The ceiling, walls, floor and all work surfaces must be in a good state of repair and made so that they can be effectively cleaned.
- People who are handling foods must wear suitable protective clothing, such as aprons.
- Temperature control is important to prevent food poisoning, either by killing off bacteria (e.g. through cooking) or reducing the multiplication of bacteria (e.g. through refrigeration).
- There should be a regular regime of cleaning and disinfection. Cleaning is the process where visible dirt, grease and food debris are removed. Disinfection is the process where bacteria are reduced to safe limits.
- Food equipment and utensils should be made of smooth, non-absorbent materials that are free from spaces where food could be trapped.
- Rubbish must be removed from the kitchen regularly.

17 Disability Discrimination Act 1995, s21.
18 The Food Safety (General Food Hygiene) Regulations 1995, Schedule 1, chapter 1.

If food is prepared regularly it is worth the PCC ensuring that someone is responsible for the kitchen and that they have taken a basic food hygiene course. They can then ensure that basic rules are followed.[19] Basic food hygiene courses are readily available throughout the country. Your local Environmental Health Department (part of your District or Borough Council) should be able to help you find one that is accredited, and there are a number of suppliers retailing computer-based packages.

In many cases, you will need to register with your local Borough or District Council's Environmental Health department.[20] It is a requirement to register when food is being handled for five or more days in any five consecutive weeks. This is free and must be done 28 days before you use the kitchen. Weekly coffee mornings would therefore come within the scope of these registration requirements. Note that there is an exemption from registration where food is being prepared occasionally by individuals or groups for gatherings or for sale at charitable events.[21] This includes coffee mornings and charity sales, provided the event is not regular. When you have registered, you can expect to be visited by someone from the department who will look around your premises and give you some useful advice on food safety issues. They will also classify the kitchen depending on the risk, which is used by them to work out how often they need to visit.

Insurance

Part of the church's responsibility in the area of health and safety is to ensure that there is proper insurance in place.[22] There are several companies who understand the insurance needs of church premises, notably Ecclesiastical Insurance Group. Insurance should cover the property, fire, theft and financial loss, employer's liability (if there are any staff), and public liability.

---

19 The Food Safety (General Food Hygiene) Regulations 1995, Schedule 1, chapter 10.

20 The Food Premises (Registration) Regulations 1991, regulation 2.

21 The Food Premises (Registration) Regulations 1991, regulation 3(3).

22 Parochial Church Councils (Powers) Measure 1956, s4.

FAQs

How can we best help ourselves in the area of health and safety?

One of the simplest ways to minimize health and safety risks is to ensure that your building is regularly maintained. A regular routine check will help. Although church fabric matters are the responsibility of the churchwardens, here is an obvious example where having a small health and safety group can help them in their work. There are various maintenance checklists available, and here is one such:

How often?	What needs to be done?
Whenever you use the building	Look around the building and check that things like fire extinguishers are in place. Check that the security fastenings on fire exits have been removed. Equipment such as toys needs to be visually inspected before use. As you leave, make sure that everything has been put away securely. Extinguish any candles and unplug electrical equipment. Check that all lights are off and the building is secured. All windows and doors should be closed.
Weekly	Test the fire alarm if there is one. Choose a different part of the system (for example a smoke detector or call point) each week. Open all fire exit doors.
Monthly	Check that safety equipment is in the right place, such as fire extinguishers and first aid kits. Test emergency lighting. Check that all doors along exit routes open without the use of a key and all fire exits are clear of obstructions. Walk around the premises – both inside and out – and ensure that there are no new hazards or maintenance issues that need to be corrected.

Six-monthly	Check the self-closing mechanisms of self-closing doors and the release mechanism of automatic fire doors. Test emergency lighting for one hour.
Annually	Have fire extinguishers tested and inspected – you should get a certificate that shows that this equipment has been checked. Test and inspect any fire detection and alarm system. Ensure that electrical appliances are tested. (Some appliances need to be tested more frequently.) Heating systems need to be serviced. (For gas systems, this must be done by a CORGI-registered gas installer competent to work on non-domestic systems.)[23] Check that exit signs are in the right place and show the correct arrows and symbols. Inspect any grounds and memorial stones, checking that trees and fences are in good condition. Check wooden seating for signs of rotting, woodworm and other problems. Ensure that your risk assessments are reviewed and updated as needed. Have your electrical installation tested for electrical safety. (This can be reduced to once every two years for installations under five years old.)
Five-yearly	Replace battery packs in fire alarm system controllers, emergency lighting equipment and other standby supplies. You will also have an inspection of the church every five years and this is a good time to review where you have got to.[24]

---

23 Gas Safety (Installation and Use) Regulations 1998.

24 This suggested list is taken from the ChurchSafety web-site with permission. There are other lists; see for example, Graham Jeffrey, *The Churchwarden's Year*.

What are typical safety issues for churches?

Here are some common safety issues in churches. Most of the tips are easy and free to put into place immediately.

- Ensure that lighting is adequate.
- Use candles carefully.
- Store items below shoulder height to prevent things falling onto people.
- Chairs should not be stacked too high otherwise they might topple.
- Don't store anything close to boilers, heaters or other heat-producing equipment.
- Secure areas of the building where people should not be permitted (such as towers).
- Always make sure that exits and fire exits are clear of obstructions.
- Don't prop open self-closing fire doors.
- Balconies should have suitable handrails or balustrades.
- Restricting hinges or locks should be fitted onto any window above ground level.
- Keep cleaning chemicals and other substances in a locked cupboard.
- Potentially dangerous equipment such as lawnmowers, ladders and other maintenance tools need to be maintained and stored securely.
- Take care that trailing cables are not a trip hazard.
- Wet flooring can be slippery so display a sign when the floor is wet.[25]

What happens when …

… we are a no-smoking zone?

Most churches have not allowed smoking for a long time. However, new laws banning smoking in public places came into effect

---

25 Based on advice from the ChurchSafety web-site.

in July 2007.[26] The smoking ban affects all churches and church halls and there is a requirement to display appropriate signs.[27] The rules vary in the different nations of the UK about the exact size and location of these signs, but the signs always include the internationally recognized 'No Smoking' symbol.

... we hold an event and want to sell alcohol?

The law requires that certain activities are licensed, such as the supply of alcohol and the performance of regulated entertainment.[28] This law might apply to some activities that take place in many church premises, though not in churches themselves.[29] Church halls are not exempt from the Act.

Licences are required for the sale of alcohol and for 'Regulated Entertainment'. This latter description includes:

- The performance of a play or an exhibition of a film.
- A performance of live music or any playing of recorded music.
- A performance of dance.[30]

Use of churches for such entertainment is also governed by canon.[31] This states that the minister shall take care that the words, music, and pictures are such as befit the House of God.[32] It also states that when a play, concert, or exhibition of films or pictures take place in a church the minister should consult the local or other authorities concerned with the precautions against fire and other dangers required by the law.[33] In other words, the canons require that the public law is obeyed.

---

26 Health Act 2006, s2.
27 Health Act 2006, s6, Smoke Free (Signs) Regulations 2007, regulation 2.
28 Licensing Act 2003, s1.
29 Licensing Act 2003, s1(9).
30 Licensing Act 2003, s1.
31 Canon F16.
32 Canon F16(1).
33 Canon F16(3).

When any 'regulated entertainment' is performed in the presence of an audience, and for the purpose of entertaining the audience, a licence is required. Worship is not covered by this legislation, therefore a premises licence is not required for that alone.

There are two types of licence. One, called a Temporary Events Notice (TEN), is intended for one-off special events and can be used where a full premises licence is not practical or not necessary.[34] This might be, for example, a one-off film night or barn dance. The fee is currently £21 for a TEN and the TEN is in the name of an individual. The TEN is submitted to the council and the police no later than ten days before the event. The paperwork is quite simple.

For those premises that are regularly used for regulated entertainment, a Premises Licence should be applied for.[35] Premises Licences do not expire and are not subject to any reviews, provided there are no complaints made to the police and local authority. To obtain a licence, an application form is completed and submitted to the local council. The fees for licences are usually waived for churches. Most active churches will find it better to apply for such a licence. These same licences cover the sale of alcohol, and the old system of applying for a temporary justices licence is no longer used.

Resources you should have at your fingertips

- Health and Safety Policy.

- Risk Assessment.

- Log Book.

Useful links

- General advice is available at the Health and Safety Executive web-site at www.hse.gov.uk/risk

---

34 Licensing Act 2003, ss99–110.
35 Licensing Act 2003, ss11–59.

- There is a lot of useful insurance advice on the Ecclesiastical Insurance Group (EIG) web-site at www.ecclesiastical.com/ourproducts/insurance/churchinsurance/index.aspx including information on health and safety policies, risk assessment, fire risks, church security, and others.

- Useful fire safety guidance is available at www.communities.gov.uk/fire/firesafety/firesafetylaw/aboutguides

- The ChurchSafety web-site is a useful and wide-ranging site focusing especially on these issues as they apply to churches: www.churchsafety.org.uk

22

Data Protection

A possible scenario

The minister keeps notes of his pastoral visits. The PCC has email addresses on the electoral roll. The parish office keeps wedding, baptism and funeral records for the purpose of follow-up. The churchwardens keep a handbook of local contractors. What does the Data Protection Act apply to and who should take any steps to make sure that you are legal?

What you need to know

The Data Protection Act 1998

This Act affects every parish. It is designed to protect the rights of individuals concerning information about them (known as *personal data*). It covers basic factual information (such as names and addresses) and expressions of opinion (such as in references). The Act doesn't guarantee personal privacy at all costs, but aims to strike a balance between the rights of individuals and the sometimes competing interests of those with legitimate reasons for using (called *processing*) personal information.[1] It applies to some paper records as well as computer records.

The Act works in two ways. First, it states that anyone who processes personal information must comply with eight principles, which make sure that personal information is:

- Fairly and lawfully processed.
- Processed for limited purposes.

---

1 Data Protection Act 1998, s1.

- Adequate, relevant and not excessive.
- Accurate and up to date.
- Not kept for longer than is necessary.
- Processed in line with your rights.
- Secure.
- Not transferred to other countries without adequate protection.[2]

The second area covered by the Act provides individuals with important rights, including the right to find out what personal information is held on computer and most paper records.[3] Should an individual or organization feel they are being denied access to personal information they are entitled to, or feel their information has not been handled according to the eight principles, they can contact the Information Commissioner's Office for help.

Compliance with the Act

This short checklist will help you comply with the Data Protection Act. Being able to answer 'Yes' to every question does not guarantee compliance, and you may need more advice in particular areas, but it should mean that you are heading in the right direction.

- Do I really need this information about an individual? Do I know what I'm going to use it for?
- Do the people whose information I hold know that I've got it, and are they likely to understand what it will be used for?
- If I'm asked to pass on personal information, would the people about whom I hold information expect me to do this without their express permission?
- Am I satisfied the information is being held securely, whether it's on paper or on computer? And what about my web-site? Is it secure?
- Is access to personal information limited to those with a strict need to know?
- Am I sure the personal information is accurate and up to date?

---

2 Data Protection Act 1998, s4.
3 Data Protection Act 1998, s7.

- Do I delete or destroy personal information as soon as I have no more need for it?
- Have I trained my staff in their duties and responsibilities under the Data Protection Act, and are they putting them into practice?
- Do I need to notify the Information Commissioner, and if so, is my notification up to date?[4]

Do I need to notify (register), and if so, how?

Notification used to be known as registration and is the process whereby a data controller informs the Data Protection Commissioner (DPC) that they are processing (handling) personal data.[5] Each incumbent and each PCC is considered to be a data controller since they are separate legal entities who will be processing personal data.

Each needs to decide whether they need to notify. It is thought that PCCs should usually be exempt from notification. This is on the assumption that they any data held by PCC officers is purely factual, such as electoral roll information or the accounts package used by the treasurer, and is therefore exempt from notification. If the PCC employs staff they will still not need to notify so long as the information they keep is used only for staff administration.

Incumbents (or priests-in-charge) should not need to notify *unless* records of pastoral care discussions (relating to beliefs, relationships, opinions, etc. rather than dates of birth/baptism and other factual information) are held on computer. It should be stressed that, even if the PCC and/or incumbent are exempt from notification, the remainder of the Act still applies to them and to everyone in the parish handling personal data.

What are subject access rights and how do they operate?

An individual has the right to receive a copy of most paper-based information held about them by that organization ('data control-

---

4 From the Information Commissioner's web-site.
5 Data Protection Act 1998, s18.

ler') within 40 days of making that request. You may charge a fee of up to £10 for providing it. This covers all information held on computer and any correspondence and other papers from which that information might be deemed to be reasonably accessible. You do not, therefore, have to scour through minutes, etc. for any mention of the individual but you would have to produce accessible information held by any church officers.

The general principle is that as much information as possible should be shared with the individual. There are, however, limited categories of material that you may withhold from the individual in the interests of protecting the rights of other individuals to privacy and for the prevention of crime, etc. You are able to withhold any references that you have given (but not any you have received). When sharing with an individual the information that you hold about them, you must remove anything which would identify a third party. You may also be entitled to hold back information containing serious allegations (for example, of child abuse) if to reveal that information would compromise the proper investigation of those allegations. In such cases you should always seek advice from your diocesan registrar or diocesan office.

FAQs

How do I notify if I need to?

To notify, you should telephone the DPC notification helpline (01625 545740). You will be asked certain questions and then sent a form to complete and to return together with a fee. You will be asked if you have an information security policy but should not get into trouble for not having one as this is primarily aimed at larger organizations; at parish level the application of common sense should be sufficient.

Are the clergy allowed access to see their own records held by the diocese?

Yes, they would be entitled to make such a request, and may be asked for the appropriate fee.

What about information we are required to publish?

The electoral roll[6] and the results of elections[7] are required to be published by the Church Representation Rules. This is not prevented by the Act so long as only the names are published by the parish. Other information should not be published without the consent of the parties involved. This may mean having two versions of the electoral roll, one containing the information suggested in Chapter 4 and another which is published prior to the APCM containing only the names of the people on the roll.

Can't the diocese notify for all of us?

Each parish and each incumbent is a legal entity and is seen by the Act as data controller. It is not, therefore, possible to make a diocesan notification, other than for the business of the diocese itself.

Who is responsible for all this?

An incumbent is responsible for deciding whether they should notify in accordance with the above outline. In cases of uncertainty they should consult their diocesan office. A PCC should appoint someone who will be responsible for understanding and knowing what data is held in the name of the PCC and whether it means that notification is necessary.

What happens when ...

... we have a parish computer?

The same principles apply to a parish computer as to the computers of parish officers. However, it may be that a PCC needs to ensure that the data on a parish computer is secure and that only those authorized have password access to the computer. You should also have a careful regime for ensuring that data is backed up.

---

6 Church Representation Rules, rule 2(3).
7 Church Representation Rules, rules 11(9) and 13(1).

... we have a parish web-site?

Data published on a parish web-site is subject to the same duty of care as all other data. If people's names are to be published on a web-site their permission should be sought first. Also, in order to comply with the eighth principle it is important that your ISP is based in Europe.

Resources you should have at your fingertips

Data Protection Act 1998 or a simple guide to it.

Useful links

- General Information Commissioners Office, Data Protection Act section: http://www.ico.gov.uk/what_we_cover/data_protection.aspx

- 'Do I need to notify?' questionnaire: http://www.ico.gov.uk/what_we_cover/data_protection/notification/do_i_need_to_notify.aspx

Bibliography

James Behrens, *Practical Church Management* (2nd edn), Leominster, Gracewing, 2005

Rupert Bursell, *Liturgy, Order and the Law*, Oxford, Clarendon Press, 1996

The Charities Act and the PCC (3rd edn), London, Church House Publishing, 2006

James A. Coriden, *An Introduction to Canon Law*, London, Geoffrey Chapman, 1991

Norman Doe, *The Legal Framework of the Church of England*, Oxford, Oxford University Press, 1996

Norman Doe, *Canon Law in the Anglican Communion*, Oxford, Clarendon Press, 1997

Martin Dudley and Virginia Rounding, *Churchwardens: A Survival Guide*, London, SPCK, 2003

Guidelines for the Professional Conduct of the Clergy, London, Church House Publishing, 2003

Mark Hill, *Ecclesiastical Law* (3rd edn), London, Butterworths, 2007

Graham Jeffery, *The Churchwarden's Year: Church Maintenance Calendar*, London, Church House Publishing, 1994

Robert Leach, *The Church Treasurer's Handbook*, London, Canterbury Press, 2005

Lynn Leeder, *Ecclesiastical Law Handbook*, London, Sweet & Maxwell, 1997

Legal Opinions concerning the Church of England, London, Church House Publishing, 2007

Kenneth M. Macmorran and Timothy Briden, *Handbook for Churchwardens and Parochial Church Councillors*, London, Continuum, 2007

G. H. Newsom and G. L. Newsom, *Faculty Jurisdiction of the Church of England*, London, Sweet & Maxwell, 1993

David Parrott and David Field, *Situation Vacant: A Guide to the Appointment Process in the Church of England*, Cambridge, Grove Books Pastoral 65, 2005

John Pitchford, *ABC for the PCC: A Handbook for Church Council Members*, London, Continuum, 2008

Protecting All God's Children (3rd edn), London, Church House Publishing, 2004

Lindsay Yates and Will Adam, *Canon Law and the Newly Ordained*, London, Church House Publishing, 2007

Common Worship

Common Worship: Services and Prayers for the Church of England, London, Church House Publishing, 2000

Common Worship: Daily Prayer, London, Church House Publishing, 2000

Common Worship: Pastoral Services, London, Church House Publishing, 2005

Common Worship: Christian Initiation, London, Church House Publishing, 2006

Common Worship: Ordination Services, London, Church House Publishing, 2007

Common Worship: Times and Seasons, London, Church House Publishing, 2006

Common Worship: Festivals, London, Church House Publishing, 2008

Appendix

Legal Material and Sources

Statutes

Ancient Monuments Consolidation and Amendment Act 1913
Asylum and Immigration Act 1996
Baptismal Fees Abolition Act 1872
Burial Laws Amendment Act 1880
Charities Act 1993
Charities Act 2006
Children Act 1989
Children and Young Persons Act 1933
Civil Partnerships Act 2004
Criminal Justice and Court Services Act 2000
Data Protection Act 1998
Disability Discrimination Act 1995
Disability Discrimination Act 2005
Ecclesiastical Commissioners Act 1836
Ecclesiastical Licences Act 1533
Employers Liability (Compulsory Insurance) Act 1969
Employment Act 2002
Employment Rights Act 1996
Equality Act 2006
Health Act 2006
Health and Safety at Work etc. Act 1974
House to House Collections Act 1939
Licensing Act 2003
Local Government Act 1972
Marriage Act 1949
Marriage (Prohibited Degrees of Relationship) Act 1986
Matrimonial Causes Act 1965
National Minimum Wage Act 1998

Occupiers Liability Act 1957
Police, Factories etc. (Miscellaneous Provisions) Act 1916
Race Relations Act 1976
Sex Discrimination Act 1975
Sharing of Church Buildings Act 1969
Social Security Contributions and Benefits Act 1992

Measures

Care of Churches and Ecclesiastical Jurisdiction Measure 1991
Churchwardens Measure 2001
Clergy Discipline Measure 2003
Church of England (Ecumenical Relations) Measure 1988
Church of England (Miscellaneous Provisions) Measure 1992
Church of England (Miscellaneous Provisions) Measure 2000
Church of England (Worship and Doctrine) Measure 1974
Ecclesiastical Fees Measure 1986
Ecclesiastical Judges and Legal Officers Measure 1976
Ecclesiastical Jurisdiction Measure 1963
Ecclesiastical Offices (Age Limit) Measure 1975
Incumbent (Vacation of Benefices) Measure 1977
Inspection of Churches Measure 1955
Parochial Church Councils (Powers) Measure 1956
Parochial Records and Registers Measure 1978
Parsonages Measure 1938
Pastoral Measure 1983
Patronage (Benefices) Measure 1986
Prayer Book (Versions of the Bible) Measure 1965
Priests (Ordination of Women) Measure 1993
Repair of Benefice Buildings Measure 1972
Synodical Government Measure 1969

Other Church of England legal material

The Canons of the Church of England, London, Church House
    Publishing, 2000
Church Representation Rules (2006 edition), London, Church
    House Publishing, 2006
Episcopal Ministry Act of Synod 1993

Other regulations, etc.

Care of Churches and Ecclesiastical Jurisdiction Measure Code
  of Practice 1993
Charities (Accounts and Reports) Regulations 2005
Church Accounting Regulations 2006
Clergy Discipline Rules 2005
Employment Equality (Religion or Belief) Regulations 2003
Employment Equality (Sexual Orientation) Regulations 2003
Faculty Jurisdiction Rules 2000
Fire Precautions (Workplace) Regulations 1997
The Food Premises (Registration) Regulations 1991
The Food Safety (General Food Hygiene) Regulations 1995
Gas Safety (Installation and Use) Regulations 1998
Health and Safety (First-Aid) Regulations 1981
Health and Safety (Information for Employees) Regulations
  1989
The Management of Health and Safety at Work Regulations
  1999
Regulatory Reform (Fire Safety) Order 2005
Smoke Free (Signs) Regulations 2007

Index